NEEDLEWORK IN MINIATURE

Also by Virginia Merrill with Thelma R. Newman

The Complete Book of Making Miniatures

Pause . . .
    in the busy pace of life
    to look at little things.
Feel the delicate texture.
Savor the minute detail.
Thrill to the authenticity.
Enjoy the precision of scale.
Then . . .
    take a needle
    and stitch a miniature.

                  Susan Richardson

NEEDLEWORK IN MINIATURE

Techniques and Inspiration for Making Miniature Rugs, Upholstery, Pillows, Bedspreads, Bed Trimmings, Doll Clothes, and Many More

VIRGINIA MERRILL & JEAN JESSOP

CROWN PUBLISHERS, INC., NEW YORK

To Reed, Derek, Sara, and Robin
Richard, Hilary, Diana, and Heather

©1978 by Virginia Merrill and Jean Jessop

All rights reserved. No part of this book may be reproduced or utilized in any form or by any means, electronic or mechanical, including photocopying, recording, or by any information storage and retrieval system, without permission in writing from the publisher.

Inquiries should be addressed to Crown Publishers, Inc., One Park Avenue, New York, N.Y. 10016

Printed in the United States of America
Published simultaneously in Canada by
General Publishing Company Limited

Library of Congress Cataloging in Publication Data

Merrill, Virginia.
   Needlework in miniature.

   Bibliography: p.
   Includes index.
   1. Needlework. 2. Miniature craft.
I. Jessop, Jean, joint author. II. Title.
TT751.M38   746.4   77-20102
ISBN 0-517-52824-X
ISBN 0-517-52825-8 pbk.

CONTENTS

ACKNOWLEDGMENTS

Our very first and most sincere thanks must go to Brandt Aymar, our editor at Crown Publishers, who had enough faith in our concept and ideas to give us a green light on this book.

Our appreciation goes as well to Mr. Eugene Kupjack and to all the countless people who gathered their finished work together to be photographed by the camera's eye, to appear again within these pages for your enjoyment. This very precise, delicate handwork is so unbelievably small that many spent half their waking hours behind a pair of good, strong glasses and very good light.

Very special thanks also to Susan Sirkis, Susan Richardson, Mitzi Van Horn, Jacqueline Andrews, Barbara Cosgrove, Cookie Ziemba, Dolores Sweatt, Hilary Jessop, Carol Dinkel, Catherine Callas Knowles, Rita Reher, Mary Fry, Marian Stannard, Barbara Bergrath, Pat Wyeth, and Judee' A. Williamson, for sharing their knowledge and their expertise in this fascinating art of expression with a needle. A book is never a good book, without the faithful, "on time" results of the film-processing expert. Our magic man is Norm Smith, and we are most grateful for his part in this book and his careful handling of our photographic material.

And most important, to our husbands, children, grandchildren, friends, and dogs for their patience and understanding at a time when the authors were so rapt and enwrapped in the creation of their favorite book.

Virginia Merrill
Jean Jessop

All photographs by Virginia Merrill unless otherwise credited

PREFACE

There are two very old crafts that form a natural combination: creating miniature furniture and petit point. Needlepoint goes back so far in time that it is difficult to say when or where it originated. Miniature furniture was found in the ruins of Rome, and no doubt, long before Rome, a child made a stone bed with leaf covers for a stick doll.

The first surviving dollhouses, for which miniature furniture was made, were built in the fifteenth century. In the sixteenth century when the idea really caught on and houses were made for children, a large number of furniture pieces and accessories were available. By the seventeenth century, the collecting of such furniture and dollhouses had spread to adults. Small fortunes were spent by collectors to commission the making of very ornate houses and rooms. The people working on these houses were highly skilled artists and craftsmen. The early houses that have survived are marvelous illustrations of life in those days. Fortunately, they have found their way to museums in Europe and England.

The fancy for small things has never lagged through the years down to this day. Perhaps we are escaping from the grim realities into a lovely, lost, small, sane world of our own making. The collecting disease is rampant.

Along with collecting goes the desire to make the miniatures as perfect as possible. In many cases this has been achieved. Two outstanding examples of near perfection come to mind. The Thorne rooms, at the Art Institute of Chicago, are magnificent miniature reproductions of over fifty rooms, each done in a different style of decoration and furnishing. Queen Mary's Dolls' House at Windsor Castle in England is a grand house, showing in detail the interiors and arrangements for royal life in the early 1920s. The beauty, fine detail, and execution of these rooms is incredible. You should not miss an opportunity to see them.

A collection of any kind is a very personal thing. It may be similar to others, but as it grows it will assume the style and reflect the taste of the collector. This is what sets it apart and makes collecting so fascinating.

Many things are massed produced now and beautifully produced. Nevertheless, there is an urge to have one-of-a-kind objects as evidenced by the staggering prices of rare, old ones. The simplest, least expensive way to achieve the unusual piece is to create your own. For the miniaturist, reproducing fine furniture well is difficult, often requiring special tools and great skill, not to mention patience.

Miniature needlework allows one to explore the joys of expression without a large outlay of money or time. As the beginner becomes more proficient in the adaptation of designs and colors, there is an ever-increasing satisfaction in one's creations. The pieces become an important part of the collection, making it truly unique and personal.

We started creating miniature needlework because of an interest in miniature furniture and rooms. We had our own high standards of workmanship and design so the plunge into making things for ourselves was logical and irresistible. We had to do our own designing and thrash out problems such as how to finish a rug with a thin edge so that the furnishings would not tilt or how to fit a design on an inch-square chair seat.

Virginia Merrill came to this work by way of the miniature world. She constructed her own rooms and fine furniture, then applied the finishing touches. Jean Jessop entered the miniature world by another route, through "normal" needlepoint. She made a petit point rug as a gift for a friend with a dollhouse. Mutual friends then got us together, and the result is here.

We both have husbands, homes, families, and businesses. Gini has two grown children, grandchildren, and a thriving business in miniature furniture, accessories, and petit point. Jean has four children, the assorted animals that go with same, and makes miniature needlepoint to order. We hope to share our enthusiasm for this work with you.

A technical note should be inserted here to define the terms "needle-point" and "petit point." Do not let the term petit point frighten you. Although it sounds terribly elegant and complicated, it is simply needle-point worked on canvas eighteen threads to the inch or finer. The name comes from the French and means "small dot." For the purposes of this book, the terms are interchangeable as everything here is needlepoint done on canvas eighteen threads to the inch or finer, hence it is all petit point.

The possibilities in miniature needlework are endless. From rugs to chair covers, bellpulls, samplers, tiny purses to lay on a table, and on and on. Once you scale down your eye and start thinking small, the imagination takes flight. Almost anything big can be made small. A bellpull or purse, done on #38 silk gauze, is delicate and satisfying, and because they are so small, they can be carried and worked on anywhere. But if you are not careful, these pieces can also be easily sucked up in a vacuum cleaner or lost, so keep your eye on them.

In this book we shall try to guide you in seeing the possibilities, in training your eye to the scale of one inch to one foot, and then start you on your way to making a few things.

There are so many excellent books written on the subject of stitches that we will not go into demonstrating the hundreds of variations. Because of the fineness that miniature work demands, there are only a few stitches necessary. We will show you how to do these. A prior knowledge of and experience in needlework would be helpful of course, but with this book, the beginner can start on his or her way—not to bigger and better but to smaller and better things. We hope that the end of this book will be just the beginning of many hours of interest and pleasure.

1
EVERYTHING STARTS WITH MATERIALS

NEEDLES

Needlepoint needles, usually called tapestry needles, are blunt with a large eye. Crewel needles are sharp with a small eye. Sizes are designated by number, the higher the number the smaller the needle. For petit point we use a #24 needle on canvas that has 22 or 24 stitches to the inch. For smaller mesh canvas #25 or #26 needles are required. The smaller sizes are sometimes hard to find, but they are available through some of the shops in our Sources of Supply list at the back of the book. A #10 crewel needle is appropriate for most miniature embroidery work.

Needles are elusive to say the least. Keep a supply on hand, perhaps in a plastic pill bottle. When traveling, stick an extra needle in the tape edging of your canvas. It is so frustrating to get ready to work and find that your only needle has disappeared. Cultivate the habit of sticking the needle into your work when you stop, even if it's only for a moment.

CANVAS

Canvas sizes are quoted by the number of threads to the inch, hence, stitches to the inch. Canvas is made of a variety of materials. We use cotton canvas in the larger sizes, #22, #24, and #32, and silk gauze from sizes #24 up to #50. The silk is expensive, but you will need only a little, and most shops will sell a small piece.

Buy a good quality canvas. Hold it up to be sure it is true, that the threads do not go off at an angle. If the weave of a piece of canvas is not straight to begin with, no amount of blocking of the finished piece will correct it.

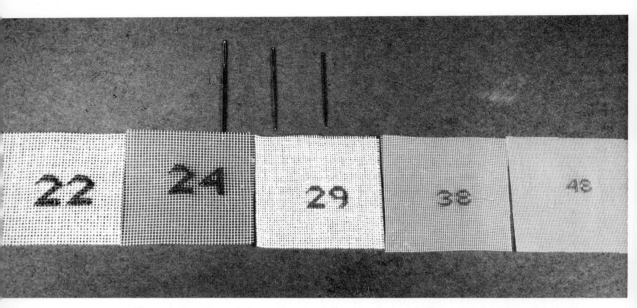

The relative sizes of the various needles, canvas, and silk gauze. Each number is 10 stitches high.

We have used only mono canvas in this book; that is, it has only one vertical and one horizontal thread for each mesh.

When buying canvas or silk gauze, do not forget to buy a piece large enough to allow for a 2" margin all the way around your work.

Canvas can be kept clean and dust-free when stored in a plastic bag.

THREAD

There are so many appropriate threads available for miniature work that it is impossible to cover them all. We have a wealth of domestic and imported materials, and the quest for them can become a hobby in itself.

First, a few general suggestions. Remember that all thread— cotton, wool, and silk—will darken a bit when stitched. A small shadow is cast by the stitch itself, and the color will not look quite as bright as it does in the skein.

When buying any type of thread, try to buy many shades of each color. In petit point, a large area of one color is more interesting if you can put in a few stitches at random of a lighter or darker shade of the same color. Embroidery work is greatly enhanced by the shading of your colors.

If you like the look of old pieces, a thread with little sheen or shininess, such as Appleton crewel wool, will make the colors seem more subtle. Miniature pieces do not take large amounts of thread, so you can splurge by having a great variety of colors and shades of color on hand.

Cut thread into lengths no longer than fourteen inches. Longer pieces are apt to tangle and will wear thin from being pulled through the canvas.

Now for specifics.

The wool we have used for the rugs in this book is Appleton crewel wool. It is imported from England, comes in about 360 colors and shades, and has a very low sheen to it. It can be used on #22 or #24 canvas, and for Bargello or the Gobelin stitch on smaller canvases. It is growing in distribution and is available by mail order. In the wool trade, the term "loft" is used to mean the fluffiness of a particular thread. Darker colors tend to have less loft because of the dye. If a stitch looks terribly thin, just stitch over it again.

We use DMC embroidery floss for rugs and embroidery—three threads for #22 and #24 canvas, one thread on #38 silk gauze and for embroidery. Two threads are used for a Bargello or other straight stitches on #38 gauze. You must experiment with coverage. DMC has a marvelous range of colors and shades and is readily available. In rug work, embroidery floss is attractive when used for Aubussons, or rugs for which a flat look is desirable. It is not fuzzy, so it gives a very clear color line. When using two or three threads, the shades can be mixed and lend flexibility and depth to the color.

The silk that has been used for both petit point and embroidery pieces is Zwicky, imported from Switzerland. There are many beautiful silks from England and France, but the colors in this brand are glorious—they are intense and glowing. Silk thread can be devilish to work with as it catches on every little rough spot. Compared to DMC, it is very expensive, but you won't need large amounts.

For use on the very fine silk gauzes, #48 and #50, we have found that plain sewing thread works well. The colors are almost endless, and the thread is available everywhere.

The wool, silk, and cotton threads mentioned here will give you an idea of the type and weight you will need. Keep your eyes open for materials of comparable weight. The brands mentioned are by no means the only ones suitable.

COLOR PENS AND PENCILS

Our first recommendation is to make as few marks on your canvas or cloth as possible, but there are times when marking is unavoidable in tracing drawings or marking guidelines.

Marking pens are a boon to the needleworker. However, they will show through the stitches on occasion, on quite a few occasions, unless you are careful. Buy only markers that are sold as permanent and indelible. Always test your marker on each type of canvas. Sometimes the sizing on one canvas differs from another and will affect the permanent qualities of the ink. Make all lines as fine as possible, and when marking a straight line, make small dashes along the thread, not a solid line. Use as light a color as you can, one closest to the background color.

It is difficult to find markers with points fine enough for use in miniature work. We recommend Sharpies, made by Sanford. These markers come in many colors and can be purchased individually in stationery, art, and needlework shops.

We often use color pencils instead of markers. Pencils are lighter in color and wear off as you work. The lines may also be hard to see, but you can redraw them if they get too faint. However, pencils, unlike markers, do not usually show through the stitches.

MAGNIFYING EQUIPMENT

The least expensive, most practical magnifying glass is the kind that hangs around your neck and rests in your chest. These magnifiers are available at most needlework shops or can be ordered. If you wear glasses for reading, wear them with your magnifier.

If you plan to do a lot of miniature work, a table-model magnifier, with fluorescent tubes under the rim, might be a good investment. In addition to being used for enlarging, it throws light directly on the work. There are various makes; we use the Dazor. Electrical supply houses often stock this type of lamp. (Sources listed in Supply Sources of this book.)

LIGHTING

In miniature work it is most important to have very good light. A 200-watt or even a 250-watt bulb is not too bright. Some people use a small high-intensity lamp but this can be glary. If you use one, make sure there are other lights on in the room. Direct sunlight is difficult because it casts hard shadows and is a harsh light.

4

When working for long stretches, get in the habit of looking up and into the distance once in a while in order to rest your eyes.

GRAPH PAPER

An 8" x 10" pad of graph paper is useful when following a chart and necessary when designing your own pieces. The sizes we use most often are 10 squares to the inch and 8 squares to the inch. The paper comes in many sizes, but these are the easiest to see. The 10-square paper is available in large sheets, 17" x 22", and a whole rug can be laid out on a sheet of this size.

Sometimes, when following a chart, a particular motif seems complicated. It can often be more easily understood if you copy it off on 8-square paper.

The size of a motif is readily transposed to your canvas size. If you are using #22 canvas, a design covering 20 squares on #10 graph paper will measure almost an inch when worked. On #38 canvas, it will measure about one-half inch, and so on.

BLOCKING SUPPLIES

You will need a piece of soft wood or heavy wallboard for blocking finished petit point. It does not have to be fancy. For years, Jean Jessop has used the back of a piece of Formica cut out of a counter, and Virginia Merrill uses a piece of composition board. The piece should be smooth, but it does not have to be large; 18" x 18" is a good size. You can probably find a piece of plywood or scrap lumber around your home. A cutting board sounds ideal, but this wood is usually too hard.

We each use a different method of attaching the piece to the board: Virginia uses pushpins, Jean uses a staple gun with ¼" staples. Thumbtacks can be used but make sure they are rustproof.

A sheet of graph paper taped to the board and covered with a piece of plastic wrap is handy for lining up your work. It is helpful to darken some of the lines with a marking pen.

ADHESIVES

Find a good glue made for work with fabrics—one that is thick, dries transparent, and will not bleed through to the front of the piece. We use Velverette, but there are several other brands. They can usually be found in craft shops and wherever sewing supplies are sold.

5

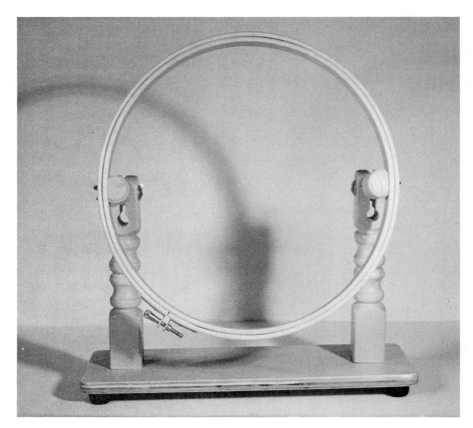

Lap embroidery hoop.

EMBROIDERY HOOPS

An embroidery hoop is really a necessity for doing pieces of embroidery. It prevents bunching and pulling the material. Inexpensive plastic or wooden hoops are made in small sizes, and more elaborate lap and floor models are available. Your material can be tacked to an artist's canvas stretcher, but a hoop is easier to use.

Some people use hoops or frames for petit point. We do not. We feel they make working awkward, and are not necessary if proper stitches and blocking techniques are used.

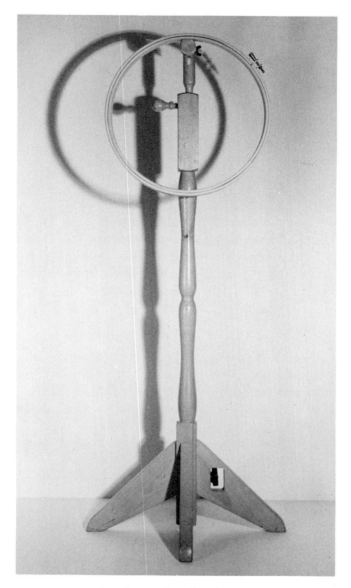

Standing embroidery hoop.

SCISSORS

There are many kinds of scissors made and sold just for needlework. However, some of them do not have sharp enough points for miniature work. Examine the points closely before buying. We have found that good cuticle scissors and a type called microscope scissors used for dissecting are very sharp. Both can be found in drugstores or surgical supply houses. You will need another pair with long, sharp blades for cutting canvas.

When you acquire a good pair of scissors, guard them, for they have a way of disappearing. The very sharp small ones are rather delicate and the points are easily bent or blunted. Put them on a long cord around your neck to keep them from sliding behind chair cushions.

THIMBLES

The use of a thimble is a matter of choice. Some people cannot work with a thimble. If you are going to do a lot of work, it is worthwhile to try to get accustomed to wearing one. The needles you will be using are fine and are apt to bore a hole in your finger after a time. Thimbles do come in sizes, so find one that fits.

MASKING TAPE

Binding your canvas with masking tape prevents the edge from raveling. It also provides a smooth edge so that your thread does not catch on exposed canvas ends. This is particularly important when working with silk thread, which is very delicate and catches on everything.

One-inch- or three-quarter-inch-wide tape is a good choice.

2
PETIT POINT

PREPARING THE CANVAS

For any piece of petit point, the canvas must have margins of 2"
on each side, so cut your canvas or gauze 4" longer and 4" wider
than the finished piece will be. Do this even when the piece will be
very small, because it will be much easier to handle when stitching
and the margins allow room for the blocking and finishing process.
Do not think of these margins as wasted material and allow yourself
to skimp.

Very small size canvas is difficult to cut on a straight line. Lay the
piece on a rather soft surface, a pile of paper or even your leg. Take
a pencil and run it firmly down the canvas where you want to make
the cut. The threads will keep the pencil within a row and give you a
straight line.

The piece of canvas has to be edged to prevent raveling. There
are several ways of doing this. You can run a line of machine
stitching along the edge, stitch seam binding over the edges, or
simply turn under as for a hem and baste. A quick method is to run
a line of glue along the edge of the canvas, but this does leave the
thread ends exposed and the yarn is apt to catch on them. The
easiest binding of all is masking tape. It goes on easily and gives a
smooth edge.

After the edges are covered, fold the canvas in quarters and mark
the center with a dot. You should very lightly mark a horizontal and
a vertical guideline with widely spaced dashes radiating from the
center. Such lines are helpful when following a chart and necessary
when designing your own piece, particularly when it comes to
doing borders. In addition, some people find it helpful to mark
guidelines every 10 rows, but this makes a lot of lines.

TRANSFERRING THE DESIGN ONTO CANVAS

Tracing a design onto petit point canvas is a very simple process since the canvas is quite transparent. If a picture appeals to you and is the wrong size, you can have it photostated and either reduced or enlarged. Look in the Yellow Pages under "Photocopying" or "Business Services." Ask for a positive print.

To make sure the drawing will be straight on the canvas, run a pencil down a row of mesh to make a guideline. You want the straight lines in the drawing to run along one thread. Hence, aligning the piece is important.

When tracing, it is a good idea to tape the original to the canvas to keep it from shifting. An easy way to do it is to put tape on the back of the original with long ends sticking out and lay it flat on a table. Now lay your canvas on that, aligning it carefully, and press it down onto the tape. Use masking tape, not cellophane tape; it holds better. Marking pens and pencils will sometimes bleed right through the canvas, so if you are tracing directly from a book or want to preserve a picture, put a piece of plastic wrap between the canvas and the original. And do not forget to test your marker for permanence on each type of canvas or gauze. Draw the lines as lightly as possible.

If you want to indicate color, you may use marking pens, acrylic paints thinned with water, or thinned oil paint. If the paint clogs the mesh, pick up the piece and blow through it gently.

CREATING YOUR OWN DESIGN

A time will come when you want to create your own designs. This will give you great satisfaction, but perhaps you will have difficulty in finding a design to suit you. The sources for ideas are endless. Start building a file of ideas cut from magazines. As you become interested, your eye will not only look at things, but it will really see them closely. You will discover that individual motifs are usually quite simple. Children's coloring books are a treasure-trove of simple line drawings. The new, more sophisticated ones often found in bookstores are a marvelous source. For flooring patterns, you will find books about rugs and embroidery in most libraries, and there is a list at the end of this book that you may find helpful. Start looking carefully at everything with a pattern. Rugs, silk scarves, wallpaper, and neckties often have beautiful designs easily adaptable to all kinds of needlework.

Direct tracing, of course, is the easiest to do, but if that opportunity does not present itself, get out your graph paper. You can draw a shape on the paper, then go back and mark the squares. Remember that a motif measuring 1" on #10 graph paper will measure a little less than ½" on #22 canvas, or a scant ¼" on #38 gauze. It will look blocky, but when it is stitched, the sharp corners and edges will soften.

It is helpful to keep a piece of miniature furniture nearby when designing. The small scale of things presents problems, and too many miniature pieces have designs that are out of proportion. The piece of furniture will keep that 1" to 1' scale firmly in mind.

Most of our rugs were designed as we stitched. We started in the center and, in effect, painted the canvas with thread. With some designs it is necessary to work the main border first as the individual motifs have to meet perfectly on the corners, for instance, the swastika borders of a Chinese rug. On most rugs you can work borders from the center out and "cheat" on the corners. When working a border, start at the center of each side and work almost to the corner. Stop. Work all four sides, then go back and cope with the corners. As you look carefully at pictures of rugs, you will notice that the borders often do not meet perfectly. Flowers or geometric motifs can be used to fill the empty space.

Colors are the most fun. Trust your own eye and taste. If you produce a disaster, the child down the block will love it, and in the process you will have learned much. When pulling colors for a project, enjoy yourself. We sometimes take out all the colors of a particular yarn or thread, throw them on the floor, then sit down and play with them, trying different combinations.

There are a few things to keep in mind. Pure white and pure black are harsh colors (you do not often see them in nature) and we rarely use them. A very dark brown, blue, or green serves for black and is softer. Off-white is also softer. Incidentally, you will be amazed at the shades of white or near white that are available. Try all your chosen colors together. They will often look quite different in relation to each other than they did by themselves. Remember, too, that colors darken a bit when stitched. Do not be bound by rules. If a combination pleases you, use it.

THE STITCHES

There are three important stitches used for making petit point. They are the Basketweave, sometimes called the Diagonal Tent; the Tent, or Continental; and the Gobelin, so called because it looks like woven tapestry. The variations of these basic three are almost endless, and many excellent books are available describing the variations. Because of the need to keep miniature pieces very fine and thin, a great number of elaborate stitches are not suitable.

The most important stitch to learn is the Basketweave, so called because of the basketlike pattern formed on the back of the work. We cannot stress enough the use of this stitch when possible. The reason for this emphasis is that the Basketweave does not pull your piece out of shape as the Continental stitch does. As you become accustomed to doing the stitch, you will find that you use it for very small areas, and the Continental stitch will be used only for odd stitches.

If you are new to needlepoint, we suggest you buy a piece of #10 canvas and learn the stitches on that. When you become proficient, switch to the finer petit point sizes.

On these diagrams the number itself indicates where the needle comes up from the back of the canvas. The tip of the arrow is where the stitch ends and the needle goes in. The crossed lines of the diagram correspond to the threads of the canvas.

The Basketweave, or Diagonal Tent, Stitch

Most people find the Basketweave awkward at first. As you become adept through practice, you will discover that it has a pleasant rhythm and obviates the need to keep turning your work. The Basketweave is always worked from the upper right-hand corner.

When you are working down a row, your needle is vertical, and the stitch on the back of the canvas is vertical too. When working up a row, your needle is horizontal as is the stitch on the back. This is important to know because if you do two down rows together or two up rows together, you will have a permanent ridge. When you have left off work for a while, always look at the back to see how your next row should go.

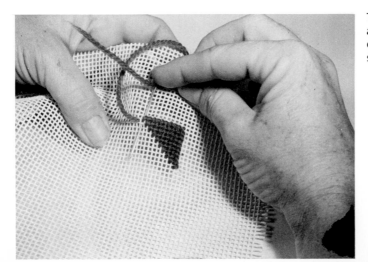

The position of the needle and thread when starting a down row of the Basketweave stitch.

12

The underside of the Basketweave stitch, showing the direction of the stitches after finishing a down row.

Beginning an up row of the Basketweave stitch. Note the direction of the needle.

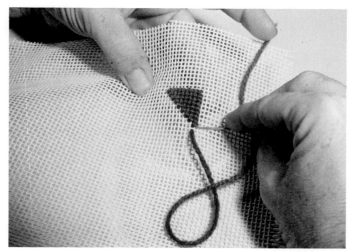

The back of the Basketweave stitch, showing the direction of the stitches after finishing an up row.

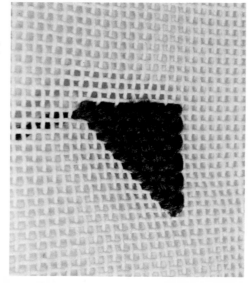

The greatest difficulty that people seem to have with the Basketweave is in changing direction at the end of a row. Look at the diagram; you will notice that #2 is directly under #1, and #4 is directly to the left of #3. At the end of a down row you make an extra stitch, coming up directly under the last stitch in the row, i.e., #1 and #2, #6 and #7, #15 and #16. At the top of an up row you make a stitch coming up directly to the left of the last stitch in the row, i.e., #3 and #4, #10 and #11, #21 and #22. This is the pivot stitch.

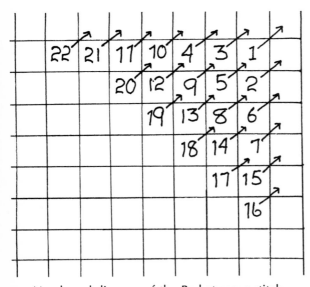

Numbered diagram of the Basketweave stitch.

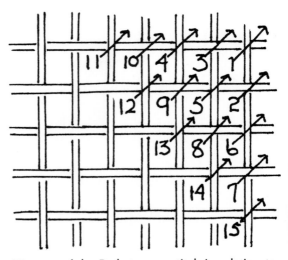

Diagram of the Basketweave stitch in relation to the canvas.

There is a right and a wrong way to work the Basketweave in relation to the canvas. The right way gives a smoother look to the finished piece. The canvas is a simple weave, over and under (this does not apply to interlocking canvas). When starting work, make each stitch on an up row cross a horizontal top thread of the canvas. On the down rows cross a top thread going vertically. The easiest way to figure it out is to study the diagram carefully. There is a ridiculous image to keep in mind:

> Harry rises horizontally.
> Vera sinks vertically.

This rule is extremely useful when doing a piece with many small, scattered motifs. No matter where you leave off on one side, then meet on the other side of a motif, your rows will be going in the proper direction. Just remember Harry and Vera.

14

The Continental, or Tent, Stitch

This stitch is the Basketweave done on a horizontal line. It should be used only for an outline in odd, small places. Unfortunately, it is often taught as the basic needlepoint stitch, and people end up with a parallelogram instead of a square or a rectangle. You work the rows from right to left so you must turn the piece 180° on alternate rows. The upside-down numbers on the diagram indicate where the work has been turned. When bringing your needle up in a hole that is already occupied, be careful not to split the previous stitch. The Continental stitch may also be done vertically, as shown in the diagram.

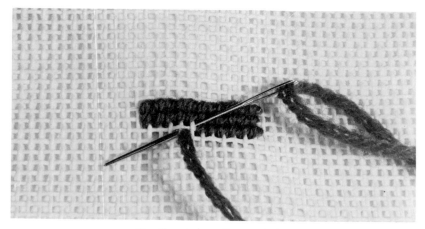

Continental, or Tent, stitch.

Numbered diagram of the Continental stitch.

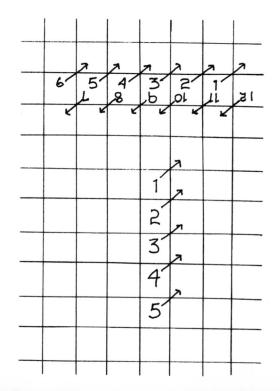

The Gobelin Stitch

The Gobelin stitch makes attractive seat and bench covers and rugs. It is usually necessary to double the number of threads used for the Basketweave for coverage with the Gobelin. The stitch is worked straight across the canvas. The Gobelin is fun to do as it covers the canvas quickly with no distortion.

In miniature work the Gobelin is often done on #38 silk gauze, since a larger canvas can throw the whole pattern out of proportion. For this same reason we do not recommend making the stitch any longer than over four threads of the canvas. On a larger sized canvas it really should be no longer than over two threads of the canvas.

The Flame, or Bargello, is the Gobelin stitch done in steps up and down to make points and curves. Examples of it and charts of patterns are shown later in the book.

The Gobelin stitch.

Numbered diagram of the Gobelin stitch.

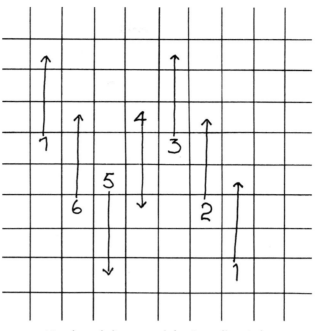

Numbered diagram of the Bargello stitch.

FOLLOWING CHARTS

Remember when following these charts that the squares of the graph represent a stitch, not a square of mesh on the canvas. The only time that this does not apply is in the charts for Bargello pieces. In these the lines of the chart correspond to the threads of the canvas.

Refer to the photograph of the finished piece often. We have included them to help you keep the overall design in mind while working. Work the motifs first, then the background.

On some of the charts we have left backgrounds blank, and the code colors that are to be used are indicated on only a small section by symbols or by the number of the color. We have done this to make the charts less confusing to follow. Where possible, we have charted a half or a quarter of a rug. This allows room to print the chart large enough to be easily read.

You can start anywhere you wish but will probably find it easiest to start with the central motif.

The number following the color indicates the particular shade used.

CHARTED RUG DESIGNS

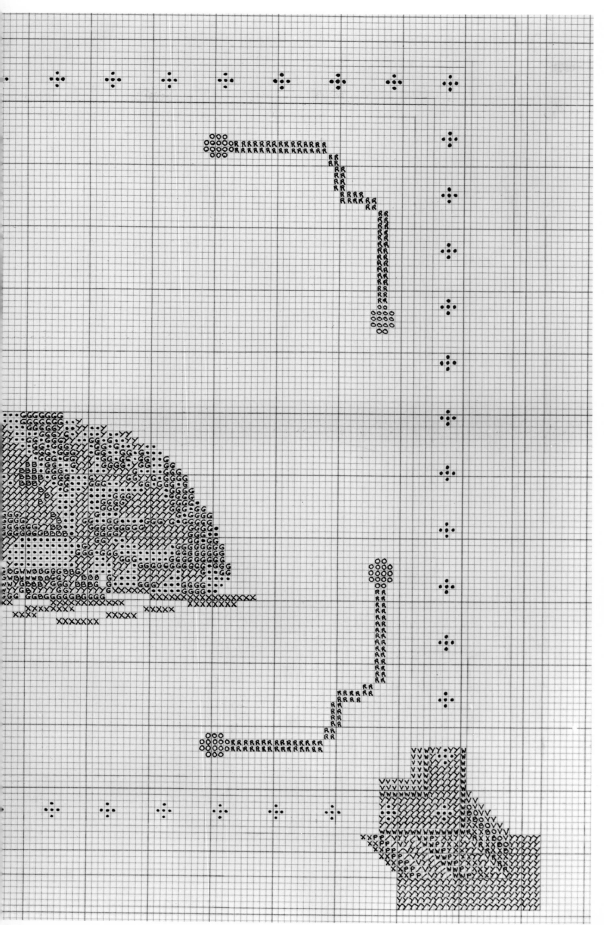

Tiger Rug

Finished size 5¼" x 7½"

#29 silk gauze
DMC cotton, 2 threads
G   Gold 832
Y   Light Gold 834
•   Black 310
W   White
B   Beige 644

/   Dark Green 937
X   Light Green 471
R   Rust 632
O   Red 3328
V   Blue 931
P   Pink 761
Background Ecru

The colors in the outer diagonal-striped border were charted at random, using a combination of colors in the rug and adding a variety of other compatible shades. Please note the change in direction of the stripes at the centers of the top and bottom and two sides of the rug. A partial diagram of the border has been worked for your convenience.

Tiger rug.

Leopard Rug

Chart for leopard rug.

Finished size 7½" x 8¼"

Continuation of chart for leopard rug.

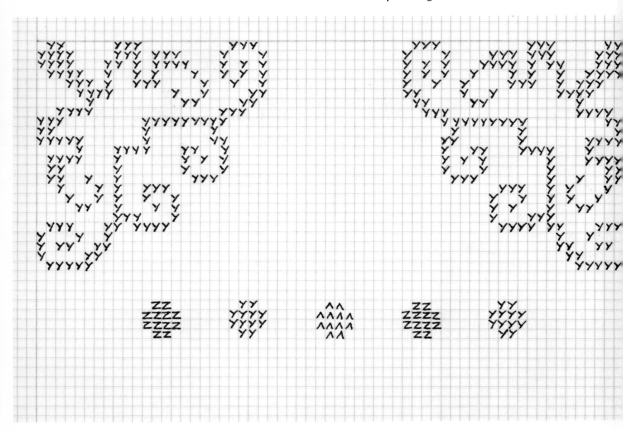

#29 silk gauze
DMC cotton, 2 threads
G Gold 676
● Black
O Olive 730
   (background area around leopard)
Y Yellow 677
Z Pink 225

R Rose 224
Λ Light Blue 928
B Dark Blue 813
/ Dark Green 937
V Light Green 3053
   (outer background)
W Snow White
T Brown 840

This rug is very flexible as to size. The finished measurement, as noted above, may be changed according to the size desired, by adding more background, filling in the four corner designs, and finishing the border edge.

Leopard rug.

Turkish Rug

Finished size 6″ x 7¼″

Chart for Turkish rug.

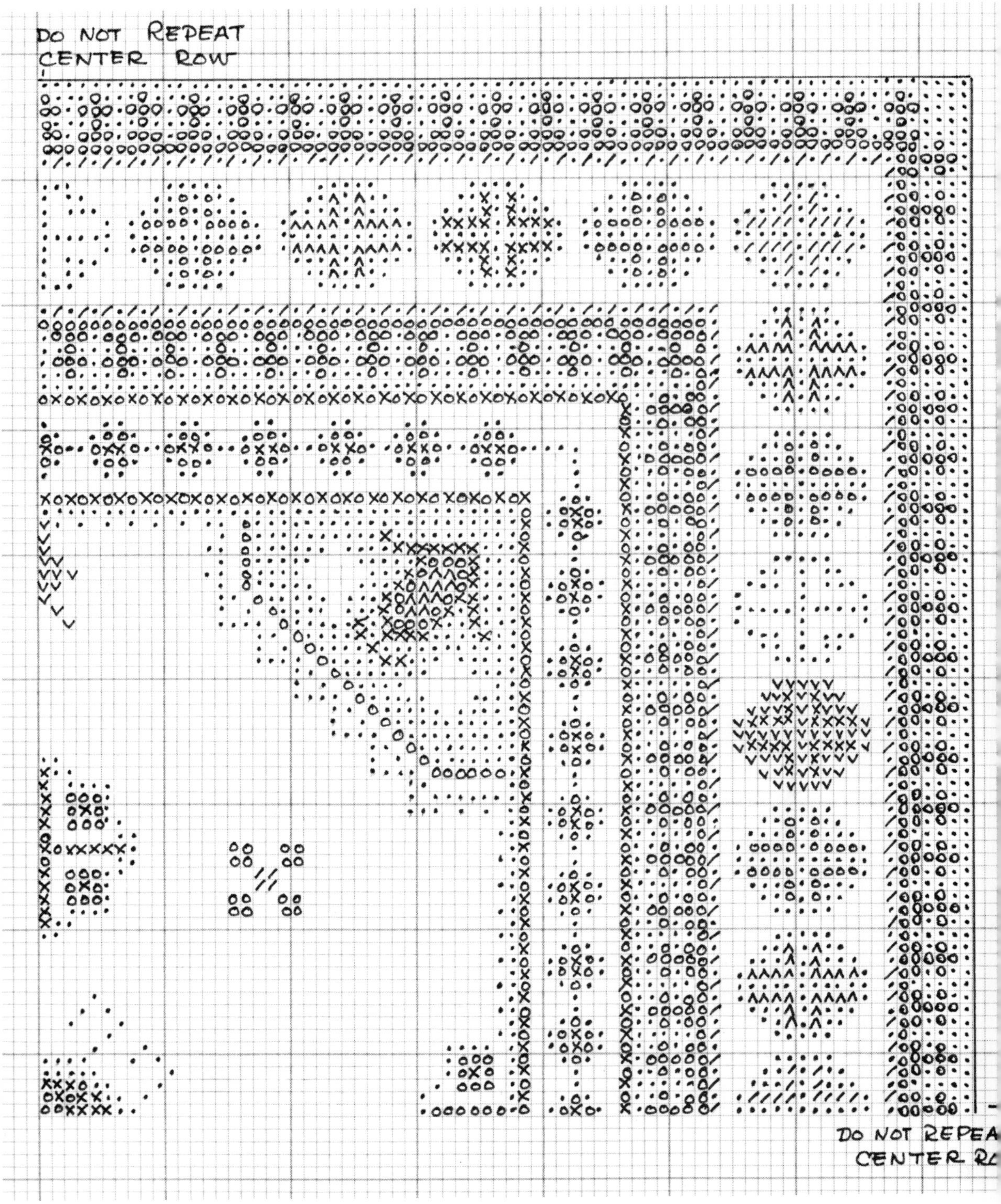

DO NOT REPEAT CENTER ROW

DO NOT REPEAT CENTER ROW

#24 canvas
Appleton crewel wool, 1 thread
. Bright China Blue 740–8
o Coral 860–5
x Flesh 700–1
v Grey Green 350–7
/ Sky Blue 560–5
^ Honeysuckle 690–4
Background Honeysuckle 690–2

Rugs of this type are often referred to as Holbeins, because they appear in so many paintings by Hans Holbein the Younger. The motif in the center is a stylized tarantula, thought by the Mongols to ward off evil.

Turkish rug.

Chart for Chinese rug.

DO NOT REPEAT
CENTER ROW

Chinese Rug

Finished size 5½" x 4"

#22 canvas
Appleton crewel wool, 1 thread
 o Honeysuckle   690–4
 x Autumn Yellow   470–1
 . White   992
Background Bright China Blue   740–8

   The center motif here is the "Eternal Knot," one of the eight Buddhist symbols of happiness.

Chinese rug.

Samarkand Rug

Finished size 6" x 8"

Chart for Samarkand rug.

DO NOT REPEAT
CENTER ROW.

#22 canvas
Appleton crewel wool, 1 thread
o Fawn 910–6
. Coral 860–3
v Coral 860–5
/ Coral 860–1
x Autumn Yellow 470–1
Background Peacock Blue 640–1

The dark and light shadings in the central field were worked at random as were the colors in the outer striped border. The yellow background of the inner band has been only partially indicated for ease in reading.

Samarkand was the city where East truly met West as the caravan routes passed through it. The rug shows the influence of both China and the Middle East.

Samarkand rug.

29

Chart for Chinese rug.

Chinese Rug

Finished size 7¼" x 8¼"

#22 canvas
Appleton crewel wool, 1 thread
∧   Dull Marine Blue   320–6
L   Dull Marine Blue   320–2
/   Coral   860–6
.   Coral   860–3
v   Coral   860–1
Background Autumn Yellow   470–1

The Chinese used few colors in their rugs. Yellow was the imperial color. The reds were "fruit" shades, tending to the yellow side rather than blue-reds.

Chinese rug.

Victorian Rug

Finished size 5½″ x 8″

Chart for Victorian rug.

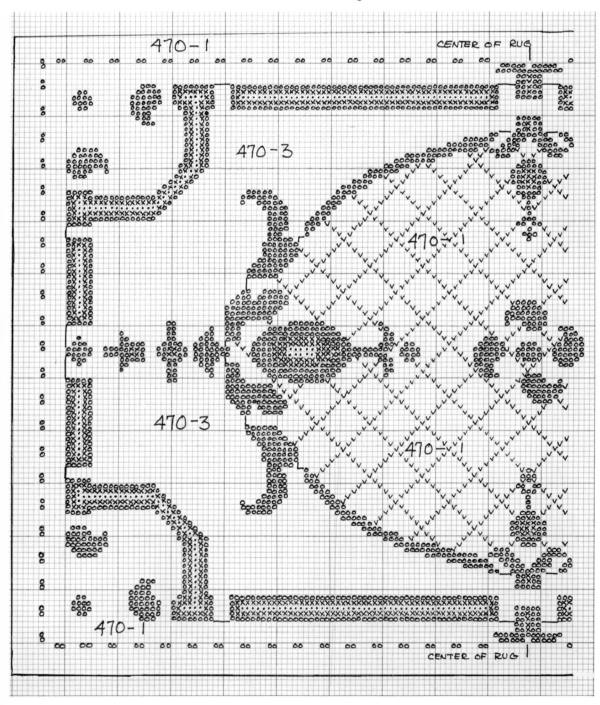

#22 canvas
Appleton crewel wool, 1 thread
o Jacobean Green 290–6
x Early English Green 540–4
. Putty Grounding 980–5
v Bright Terra Cotta 220–2
Backgrounds
Autumn Yellow 470–3
Autumn Yellow 470–1

    The background colors are noted on the chart for each area. Dark lines show where colors change.
    The basic design for this rug is from the book *Victorian Stencils for Design and Decoration*, selected by Edmund V. Gillon, Jr., Dover Publications, Inc.

Victorian rug.

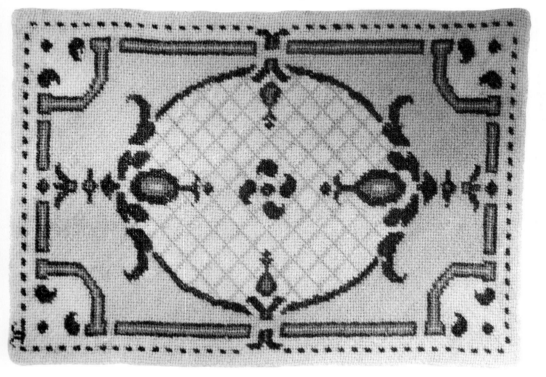

33

French Rug

Finished size 8¼" x 6"

Chart for French rug.

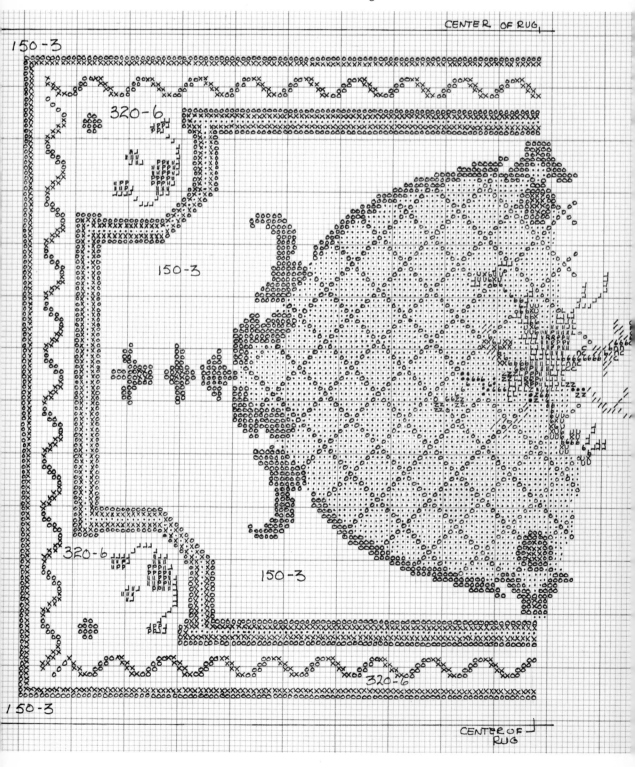

#22 canvas
Appleton crewel wool, 1 thread

ɔ	Dull Marine Blue 320–6		z	Purple 100–2
o	Honeysuckle 690–4		●	Purple 100–5
x	Autumn Yellow 470–1		x	Autumn Yellow, in flowers 470–3
.	Flesh 700–1		6	Early English Green 540–4
R	Bright Terra Cotta 220–6		L	Jacobean Green 290–6
II	Bright Terra Cotta 220–4		⌐	Grey Green 350–2
P	Rose Pink 750–2		/	Grey Green 350–7
c	Coral 860–3			Backgrounds
n	Coral 860–1			Dull Marine Blue 320–6
				Mid Blue 150–3

This rug is the same basic design as the Victorian rug. The background colors are indicated by number on the chart. Other backgrounds may be easily substituted, such as soft greens or soft roses.

French rug.

Oriental Runner

Finished size 3½" x 6¼"

Chart for Oriental runner.

#22 canvas
Appleton crewel wool, 1 thread
6   Mid Blue   150–3

o   Dull Marine Blue   320–6
.   Flesh   700–1
x   Flame Red   200–6

This runner can easily be made longer or shorter or wider by adjusting the number of small motifs in the center field.

Oriental runner.

Heriz Medallion Rug

Finished size 8″ x 10″

Chart for Heriz Medallion rug.

#22 canvas
Appleton crewel wool, 1 thread
. Bright China Blue   740–8
/ Scarlet   500–4
x Bright Terra Cotta   220–2

o Autumn Yellow   470–3
∧ Flesh   700–1
v Early English Green   540–4
● Sky Blue   560–5

One quarter of the rug is charted. The colors in the medallions of the main border are used at random. Colors of the background of large areas are noted by number.

Heriz Medallion rug.

Chart for Turkish prayer rug.

Turkish Prayer Rug

Finished size 5½" x 7"

#22 canvas
Appleton crewel wool, 1 thread
o Bright China Blue 740–8
/ Honeysuckle 690–2
L Honeysuckle 690–4
6 Sea Green 400–4

Λ Mid Blue 150–3
. Flame Red 200–4
x Flame Red 200–6
v Flame Red 200–8
+ Flesh 700–1

This rug is typical in color and design of the prayer rugs made in Anatolia. The point of the niche was turned to face Mecca during prayer. The lamp in the center symbolized Allah, "the light of the heavens, and the earth."

Turkish prayer rug.

CENTER OF RUG

Persian Rug

Finished size 9¾" x 7⅛"

#22 canvas
Appleton crewel wool, 1 thread
Δ Mid Blue   150–7
. Bright Terra Cotta   220–4
o Honeysuckle   690–4
x Flesh 700–1
6 Mid Blue   150–3
s Sky Blue   560–8
v Early English Green   540–4
⌐ Brown Grounding   580–2
/ Honeysuckle   690–2
Random shading in background of field Bright Terra Cotta   220–2

This rug, though not an adaptation of a particular style, is typically Persian, with flowers and animals.

Persian rug.

Chart for Colonial American rug.

DO NOT REPEAT
CENTER ROW ↓

Colonial American Rug

Finished size 6″ x 7½″

#22 canvas
Appleton crewel wool, 1 thread
  x Grey Green 350-7
  . Grey Green 350-2
  o Flame Red 200-5

  > Autumn Yellow 470-3
  ∪ Mauve 600-3
  \ Bright China Blue 740-2
Background Flesh 700-1

This design was adapted from a painted canvas floor covering. Such coverings were commonly used in colonial times instead of rugs.

Colonial American rug.

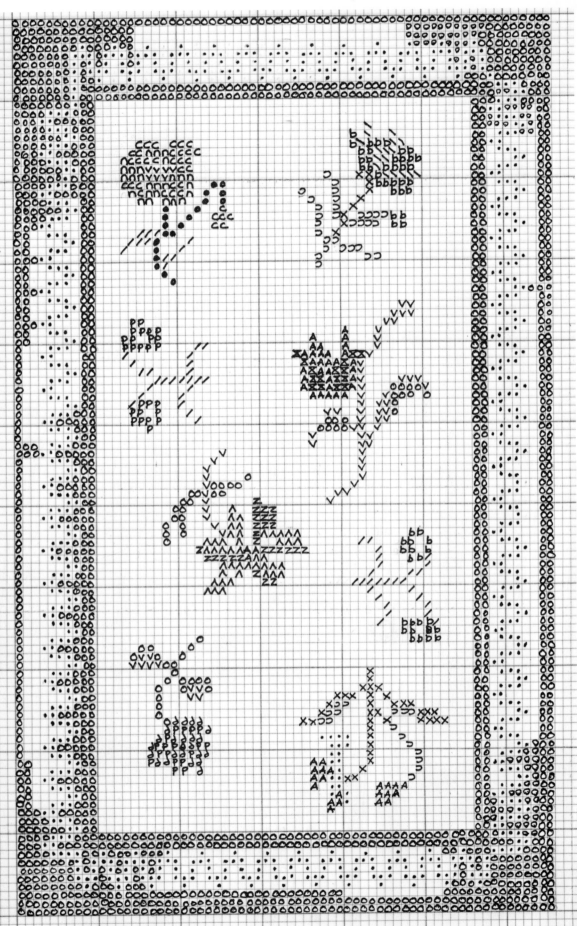

Small Flowered Rug

Finished size 2¾" x 5"

#22 canvas
Appleton crewel wool, 1 thread

Poppy

c   Coral   860–5
∩   Coral   860–6
Leaves
/   Mid Blue   150–7
●   Mid Blue   150–3

Cornflower

b   Sky Blue   560–1
\   Bright China Blue   740–5
Leaves
ɔ   Early English Green   540–1
x   Early English Green   540–4

Pink Bells

P   Pink   750–2
Leaves and Stem
/   Mid Blue   150–7

Tulip

A   Autumn Yellow   470–3
X   Autumn Yellow   470–6
Leaves
v   Grey Green   350–2
o   Grey Green   350–7

Violet

Λ   Purple   100–2
z   Purple   100–5
A   Autumn Yellow   470–3
Leaves
v   Grey Green   350–2
o   Grey Green   350–7

Blue Bells

b   Sky Blue   560–1
Leaves and Stem
/   Mid Blue   150–7

Rose

P   Rose Pink   750–2
d   Rose Pink   750–6
Leaves
v   Grey Green   350–2
o   Grey Green   350–7

Daffodil

.   Autumn Yellow   470–1
A   Autumn Yellow   470–3
Leaves
ɔ   Early English Green   540–1
x   Early English Green   540–4

Border

o   Grey Green   350–7
.   Autumn Yellow   470–1

Background of field

White   992

Small flowered rug.

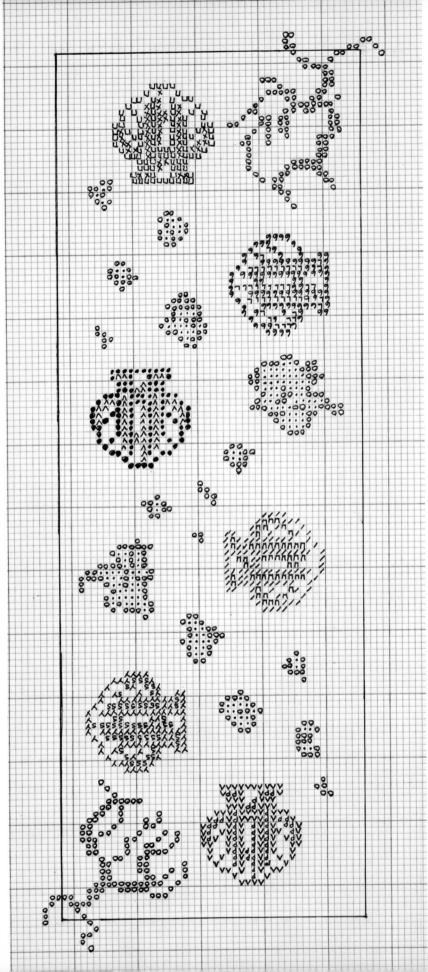

Chart for scallop shell rug.

Scallop Shell Rug

Finished size 6¾" x 3"

#22 canvas
DMC embroidery floss, 3 threads
Λ Bright Red   347
P Pink   818
Y Dark Yellow   729
s Light Yellow   677
/ Dark Blue   931
⊔ Light Blue   775
6 Dark Green   320

L Light Green   503
• Dark Purple   208
v Light Purple   210
⊓ Dark Rust   301
x Light Rust   754
o Dark Seaweed   3011
. Light Seaweed   3013
Background Ecru

Borders
6 rows of 2 threads Light Blue   932, 1 thread Darker Blue   931
4 rows of 3 threads Darker Blue   931

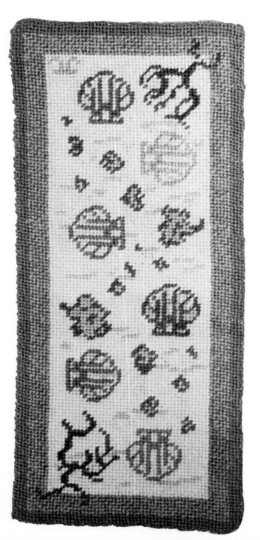

Scallop shell rug.

Chart for geometric Dhurrie rug.

Geometric Dhurrie Rug

Finished size 6½" x 8"

#22 canvas
Appleton crewel wool, 1 thread
o   Brown Grounding   580–2
.   Flesh   700–1

x   Peacock Blue   640–1
v   Fawn   910–1
p   Putty Grounding   980–5

Colors used at random in diamonds and in main border.

Peacock Blues   640–1–3
Fawn   910–1
Flame Reds   200–4–5–6
Mid Blue   150–3
Early English Green   540–4

Honeysuckles   690–2–4
Dull Marine Blue   320–6
Mauve   600–5
Putty Grounding   980–5

Do the outline of the diamonds first, then have fun with colors. Instead of our suggested colors you could use shades of all one color. Since the Dhurries are a flat weave, 3 threads of DMC embroidery floss could be used instead of Appleton wool.

Geometric Dhurrie rug.

Chart for Dhurrie rug.

—DO NOT
CENTER

DO NOT REPEAT
CENTER ROW.

Dhurrie Rug

Finished size 7⅜" x 9½"

#22 canvas
Appleton crewel wool, 1 thread
Background Flesh 700–1
  . Coral 860–3
  c Coral 860–6
  L Mid Blue 150–3
  / Bright China Blue 740–8

T Fawn 910–1
x Fawn 910–6
v Putty Grounding 980–5
o Jacobean Green 290–6
⊐ Early English Green 540–1
∧ Honeysuckle 690–4

Parts of the putty background of the "cross" border have been left blank to make the chart easier to read.

The Dhurrie rugs are a flat-weave rug made in India. The designs are marvelously adaptable for use with any type of room.

Dhurrie rug.

Chart for octagonal rug.

Octagonal Rug

Finished size 7½" x 7½"

#22 canvas
Appleton crewel wool, 1 thread
/ Bright Terra Cotta 220–6
. Bright Terra Cotta 220–4
v Bright Terra Cotta 220–2
+ White 992
x Peacock Blue 640–3
o Peacock Blue 640–1
- Fawn 910–4
z Fawn 910–1

L Bright China Blue 740–2
Λ Bright China Blue 740–5
● Bright Yellow 550–2
Δ Honeysuckle 690–4
6 Mauve 600–3
II Mauve 600–5
Background Flesh 700–1

The original of this rug is octagonal in shape, but it could easily be made square or oblong, with a simple ribbon or plain border.

Octagonal rug.

55

Chart for rug of borders.

Rug of Borders

Finished size 6½" x 10½"

#22 or #24 canvas
Appleton crewel wool, 1 thread
- o   Bright China Blue   740–8
- x   Flame Red   200–4
- >   Flame Red   200–6
- +   Flame Red   200–8

- .   Honeysuckle   690–2
- ௳   Peacock Blue   640–3
- <   Peacock Blue   640–1
- \   Honeysuckle   690–4
- ⌐   Autumn Yellow   470–3
- Background Flesh   700–1

We started this piece to illustrate a few of the many Oriental borders, and it became an attractive rug in itself. It can be made any size by subtracting borders or adding them. The length is up to you.

Rug of borders.

Little Ship Rug

Finished size 2″ x 3″

Chart of little ship rug.

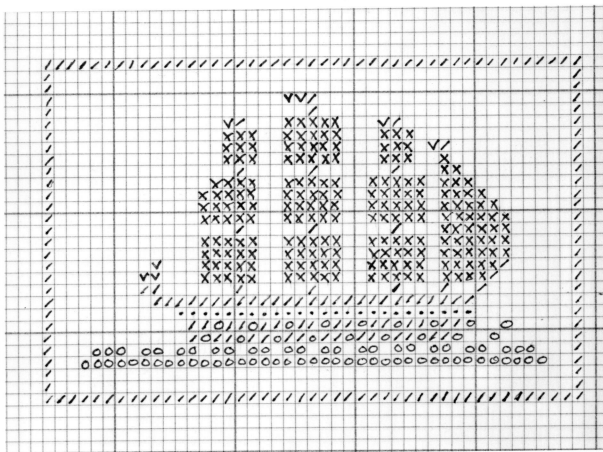

58

#18 canvas
DMC embroidery floss, 6 threads
v Red
. Gold
/ Brown
o Dark Blue
x White
Background Light Blue

This little rug was designed and made by Meg Brown.

Little ship rug.

Line drawing of Gobelin stitch rug.

Gobelin Stitch Rug

Finished size 6″ x 8″

#32 cotton canvas
Appleton crewel wool, 1 thread

This drawing is the actual size of the rug, so it can be traced directly onto your canvas. The Gobelin stitch was worked over two threads of the canvas. Be careful to keep your rows even, and do not pull the wool too tight or it will make the canvas pucker.

This design was adapted from several Portuguese rugs and the typical soft colors were used.

Gobelin stitch rug.

Animal Rug

Finished size 6" x 6½"

Chart for animal rug.

Line drawing for animal rug.

#29 silk gauze
DMC embroidery floss, 2 threads

Elephant

x   Dark Red   221
B   Black
o   Light Red   223
w   White
s   1 Black, 1 Red   221

Monkey

x   Dark Brown   3031
w   White
o   Rust   356
.   Brown   611
z   Dark Brown   612
T   Dark Green   937
L   Light Green   470

Hippo

B Black
o Blue 791
x 1 Light Blue 794, 1 Black

Lion

. Light Brown 611
z Dark Brown 3031
o Dark Gold 729
T Tan 644
/ Light Gold 677
G Dark Grey lines on rock.
   Fill in with lighter grey.

Ostrich

B Black
P Pink 223
T Tan 644
w White
Ŧ 1 Pink 223, 1 Tan 644

/ Green grass under animals 470

Border

x Brown 610
R Rust 221
/ Green 470
Background Yellow 745

Charts for the individual animals and the border are shown. The actual size drawing of the rug will help you to place the animals and foliage. We suggest laying your canvas on the drawing and tracing it. Then use the charts to work the animals.

Animal rug.

CHARTED SMALLER DESIGNS

Smaller Petit Point Pieces

These pieces are often chair seats, bench covers, and upholstery of one kind or another. When starting upholstery pieces, first trace the outline of the area to be covered on the canvas or gauze. Be sure to leave a margin of 2" around the edges. Mark the center of the design and the center of the canvas. Keep fitting the work on the piece to be covered as you stitch.

You can buy furniture already made or make the pieces from kits and cover them with your own upholstery. Be sure to make the petit point piece large enough to cover the piece of furniture.

Samplers and other wall hangings can be worked in the cross-stitch on fine silk or gauze or even-weave fabric with the background left blank. These pieces have a very delicate look and take less time to finish.

Tapestries

Tapestries, which are pictures painted with thread, were once used in houses and castles to add much-needed insulation and color to cold, gloomy rooms. Nowadays they are used for decoration. The magnificent old ones were woven, but today's are made in petit point or in a combination of petit point and embroidery stitches. Ours were all drawn directly onto the gauze, then worked with color.

Chart of leopard wall tapestry.

Leopard Wall Tapestry

Finished size 2¼″ x 3⅛″

#38 silk gauze
DMC embroidery floss, 1 thread

Sun

Y Bright Yellow 725
c Lighter Yellow 744

Sky

⌐ Blue 775
⊓ Dark leaves and border 469
+ Brown branches 610
Background Blue 828

Plants

o Dark Green 470
x Lighter Green 471

Flowers

∧ Maroon 221
P Pink 818
. White
v Red 350

Butterfly

v Red 350
o Purple 552
c Green 3031
+ Brown 610

Leopard

/ Gold 676
s Brown 611
+ Dark Brown 610
. White
6 Green Eyes 993

Leopard wall tapestry.

Bunny Stool

Finished size 1¾" x 2¼"

Chart of bunny stool.

#38 silk gauze
DMC embroidery floss, 1 thread
 T Tan 3032
 G Green 470
 / Gold 676
 Y Yellow 677
 W Ecru
 X White
 B Background Blue 311

The bunnies and flower design are worked first, filling in the blue background to fit your own particular piece. This is glued in place and the border design is worked as a separate band and glued in place around the edge of the stool. Three threads of the background blue were braided to form an edging to give the stool a neat finished edge.

Bunny stool.

Oriental Wall Hanging

Finished size 1½" x 3"

#38 silk gauze
DMC embroidery floss, 2 threads
Dark Red   347
Light Red   760
White
Green Leaves   470
Brown Stems   610
Gold Leaf and Flower Centers   676
Background Ecru
Border   671

This wall hanging was adapted from a Hiroshige painting. It was worked in the Gobelin stitch going over two threads. The drawing is the actual size of the piece, so it can be traced directly onto the gauze. Your own initials can be put in the upper left-hand corner.

Drawing for Oriental wall hanging.

70

Oriental wall hanging.

Charts for brick doorstops.

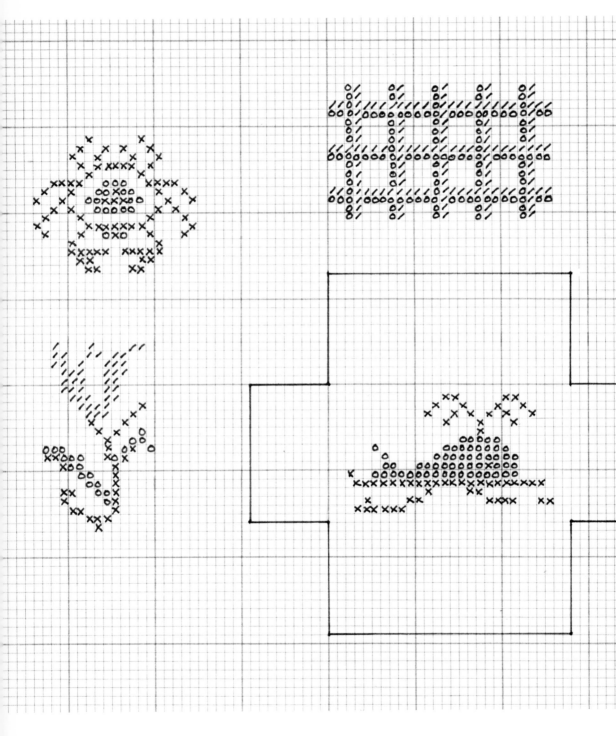

Brick Doorstops

Finished size ½″ x ¾″

#38 silk gauze
DMC embroidery floss, 1 thread

Miniature clay bricks are available from dealers, or blocks of wood can be cut to the proper size. Each of these bricks will vary a bit in size, so it is necessary to keep fitting the piece on the brick as the work progresses. The bottom does not have to be covered, but the top and sides should meet neatly on the corners.

When the petit point is completed, run a line of glue along the last row or two of the stitches; this prevents raveling. Let the glue dry thoroughly, then cut off the excess gauze as close as possible to the stitching. Glue the piece to the brick.

Shown are several brick doorstops and they should be worked in colors according to one's choice.

Brick doorstops.

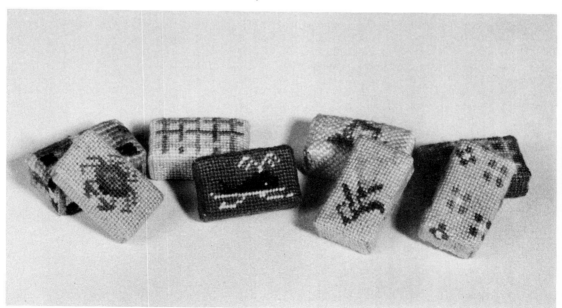

Chart for Victorian fire screen.

Victorian Fire Screen

Finished size 1¾" x 2"

#48 silk gauze
Corticelli pure silk thread and DMC embroidery floss, 1 thread
G Green 3011
/ Light Green 470
O Gold 677
V Rose 3350
● Light Rose 3354
L Pink 778
Background Corticelli Beige

Design worked in DMC embroidery floss with the background in silk. The border design is a series of three stitches worked alternately with the background color for two rows as shown on graph.

Victorian fire screen.

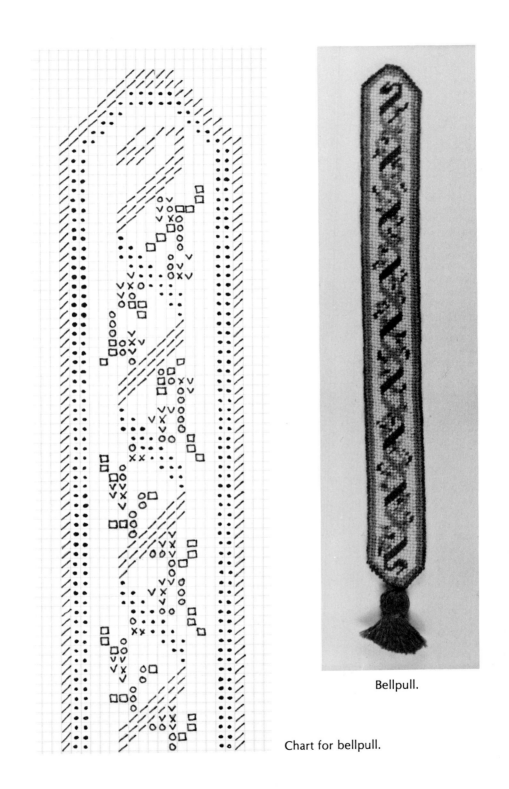

Bellpull.

Chart for bellpull.

76

Bellpull

Finished size ½" x 4½"

#38 silk gauze
DMC embroidery floss, 1 thread
Ribbon and borders
Dark Green   3052
Light Green   3052
Vine Blue Green   519
Leaves Dark Blue Green   930
Flowers
Light Pink   3354
Dark Pink   3350

When you have finished working the bellpull, press it with a steam iron. Then turn under the edges and glue them or sew them down. Sew a ring to the top for hanging, and make a tassel for the bottom.

To make a tassel, cut a strip of cardboard ½" wide and wrap it 14 turns with a thread of embroidery floss. Run a single thread of floss under all the wrapping at one side and tie as tightly as possible. Leave long ends since you will use these to sew the tassel to the bellpull. Now cut through the threads at the opposite side. You should have a bunch of threads secured in the middle. Fold at the tie, and tie another single thread around the whole tassel ⅛" below the first tie. Trim the ends so they are even and sew it to the bellpull.

Drawing for making tassel for bellpull.

77

Shell Chair Seat

Finished size of shell ⅞″ x ⅝″

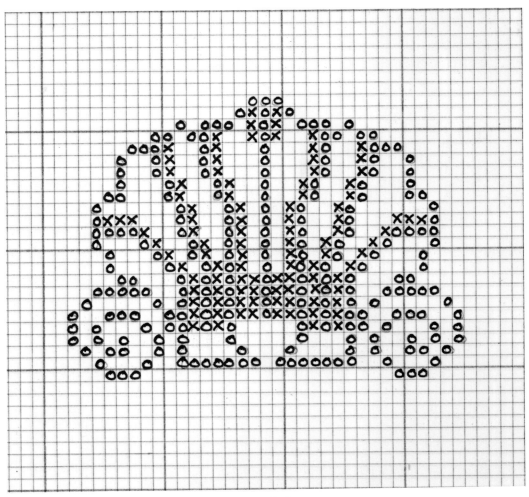

Chart for shell chair seat.

#38 silk gauze
DMC embroidery floss, 1 thread

The shell was adapted from a design made by Martha Washington for chairs at Mount Vernon. We have used a dark green and light green for the outline of the shell itself, and a light gold for the interior of the shell. The background is dark gold. The design is a most adaptable one as to color. We have outlined shells in reds, blues, and browns and used ecru for the interiors and backgrounds. The design could also be used on #22 or #24 canvas as the repeated motif for the center of a rug.

Shell chair seat.

Bargello Settee Seat

The settee seat was made on #38 silk gauze, with two threads of DMC embroidery floss over four threads of the gauze. This particular piece was worked with a rust, blue-green, dark green, and ecru. Four shades of one color, or three shades with ecru or white, would be attractive, depending on your color scheme.

Chart for Bargello settee seat.

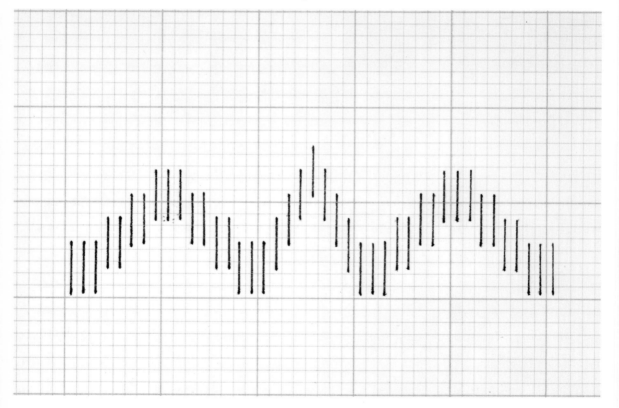

Bargello settee seat.

Tester Bed Hangings

#32 cotton canvas
Appleton crewel wool, 1 thread
Honeysuckle   690–4
Bright Yellow   550–2
White   992

This is an example of the classic Flame stitch, or Bargello. Wool was used to lend a softer look. Any range of colors can be used.

The name Bargello comes from the name of the museum in Italy where the first examples of this kind of needlework are preserved.

Chart for tester bed hangings.

Tester bed hangings.

Flowered Chair Seat Covers

Size of flowers 1″ x 1″ approximately

The original seats were worked with Zwicky silk, but another silk
or cotton may be easily substituted. The designs themselves were
adapted from drawings of English wildflowers. It would be fun to
make a set of chair seats using designs of flowers growing near your
home.

Chart for flowered chair seat covers.

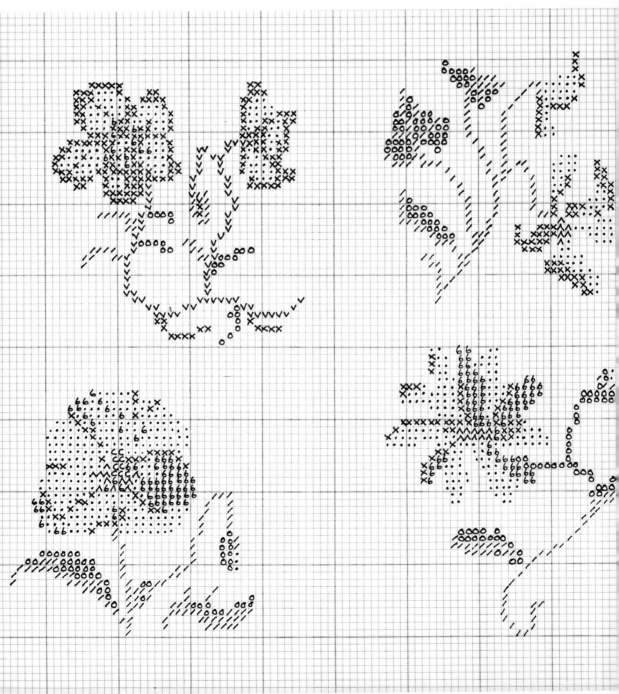

#38 silk gauze
Zwicky silk, 1 thread

Rockrose

v   Maroon   2395
/   Dark Green   2063 a
o   Light Green   2061
x   Dark Yellow   2122
.   Light Yellow   2017
6   Pink   2181
Background Beige   2323

Poppy

/   Dark Green   2063   a
o   Light Green   2061
x   Dark Red   2196
.   Medium Red   2200
6   Light Red   2181
^   Dark Green   2063   b
c   Light Green   2067
Background Beige   2323

Violet

/   Dark Green   2063   b
o   Light Green   2061
x   Dark Violet   2370
.   Light Violet   2251
^   Yellow   2122
Background Beige   2323

Black-eyed Susan

/   Dark Green   2348
o   Light Green   2067
.   Medium Yellow   2122
x   Dark Gold   2088
6   Light Gold   2011
^   Brown   DMC   611
Background Beige 2323

Flowered chair seat covers.

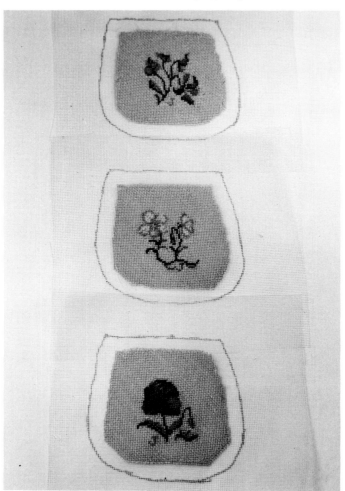

Sampler

Finished size 2¼" x 2"

#38 silk gauze
DMC embroidery floss, 1 thread
Y Yellow 746
P Pink 3354
B Blue 794
R Red 3350
G Green 3348
V Gold 834
Background Blue 311

The design is worked first, and the background filled to the desired finished size.

To stay within the bounds of the proper scale, use an overlay thread, after the background is filled in, to finish the letters B, E, K, Q, R, and X.

The sampler is then ready for framing.

Sampler.

Pole Fire Screen

Finished size 1½" x 2"

#38 silk gauze
DMC embroidery floss, 1 thread
X Gold 833
O Dark Pink 223
W Pale Pink 225
/ Pink 224

B Blue 928
– Dark Blue 931
M Med. Blue 932
Z Olive 3011
G Green 3051
Background Ecru

Work flower design, then fill in the background color to the size desired.

Chart for pole fire screen.

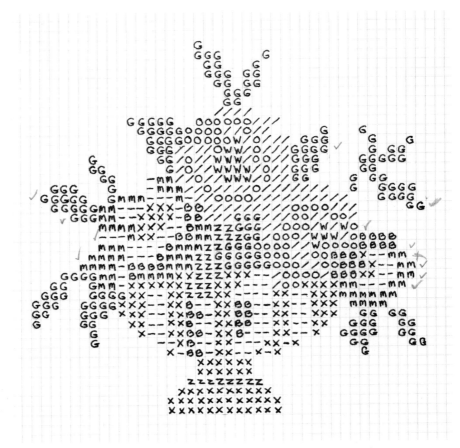

Pole fire screen.

Bird Design

Finished size 1½" x 1½"

#38 silk gauze
DMC embroidery floss, 1 thread
B   Blue   813
R   Red   356
Y   Yellow   744
G   Dark Green   3346
/   Light Green   3348
P   Pink   758
W   White
Background Ecru

This bird design is very suitable for a pillow, stool, fire screen, or for framing and can be adapted as a chair seat.

Chart for bird design.

90

Bird design.

Elephant Design

Finished size 1″ x 1½″

Chart for elephant design.

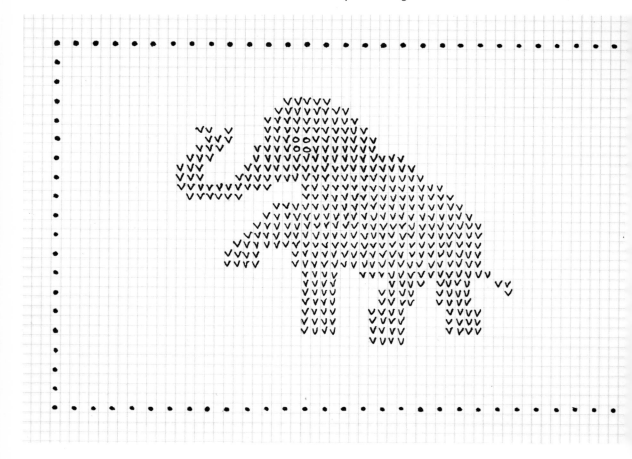

#38 silk gauze
DMC embroidery floss, 1 thread
V   Grey   415
O   Dark Grey   535
●   Red   413
Background Blue   336

Work the elephant design, the border, and then fill in the background. This may be used to cover a pillow, a stool, or may be framed as a picture.

Elephant design.

Duck Pillow

Finished size 1″ x 1″

Chart for duck pillow.

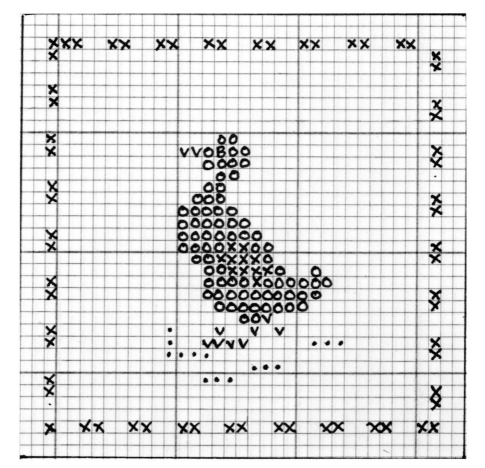

#38 silk gauze
DMC embroidery floss, 1 thread
o White
x Yellow 726
v Red 946
. Green 471
B Black (eye)
Background Navy Blue 823

Duck pillow.

Make the front of the pillow following the chart. Make a piece of the same size for the back, either plain or incorporating your initials and the date if you wish.

When the petit point has been completed, turn under the edges and sew the back and front pieces together using an overcast stitch. Leave one side open for stuffing. The stuffing may be cotton, an old piece of nylon stocking, or any bit of soft material. Be careful not to make the pillow too fat, for it will be out of proportion.

Sew the fourth side with an overcast stitch.

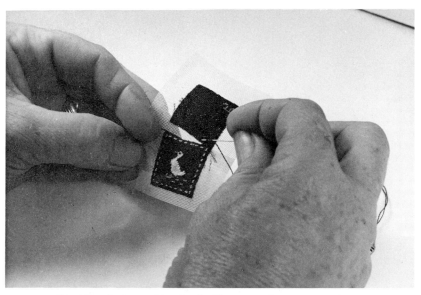

Stitching front and back of pillow together at top edge.

Stuffing cotton into cavity.

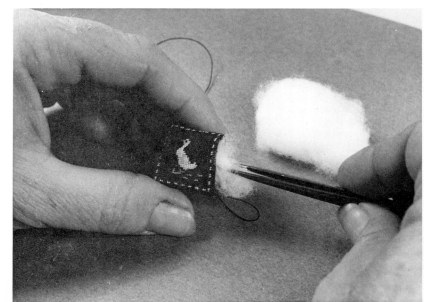

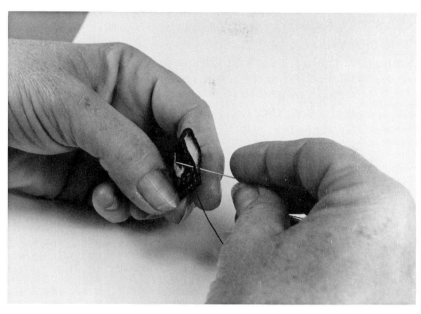

Overcast open end to secure stuffing.

RIPPING OUT NEEDLEWORK

When you have made a mistake, take your needle off the thread, turn the work over, and pull the stitch out with the needle. If you want to rip out large areas, use very fine pointed scissors, cut the stitches on the back of the work very carefully, and pull them out. A tweezer will help with very fine work. The process is extremely tedious because you must go slowly and not cut the backing. Use a magnifying glass if you have one.

MENDING CANVAS

Petit point canvas can be easily repaired, so do not despair if you cut a thread or even a hole.

For just one thread, unravel a two-inch-or-so piece from the edge of the canvas. Lay it along the damaged thread so that it extends to each side of the cut. Stitch right over the two threads. The repair will not show.

If a real hole is the problem, cut a square piece of canvas larger than the hole. Hold it in back of the original piece, lining up the threads carefully. Then stitch right through both pieces of canvas. The patch will not show, all is saved.

97

WASHING

When a piece of petit point becomes soiled, it can be washed in warm water and a mild liquid soap. It is best to do this before blocking. Be gentle and do not squeeze or wring; rather, roll the piece in a towel to get rid of the excess moisture. Then you can go ahead with the blocking process. If it has been blocked already, lay it on a flat surface and pull it into shape. When dry, it can be lightly pressed with a steam iron.

FINISHING PROCEDURES
Blocking and Shaping

Almost all needlework looks better if it is blocked or pressed upon completion. It is not difficult with these small pieces.

For petit point, use your blocking board with graph paper and plastic wrap as described in chapter 1. Wet the piece thoroughly with coolish water. Tack or staple the piece down, pulling it to conform to the straight lines on the paper. Work one side at a time and put your staples or tacks close together, a half inch or so away from the stitching. If you have a piece of canvas with a selvage on one side, clip through the selvage before blocking so that it does not pull.

Let the petit point dry thoroughly; it will take a day . If perchance the work does not look straight, block it again; twice should do it.

Leopard rug being blocked during the process of stitching.

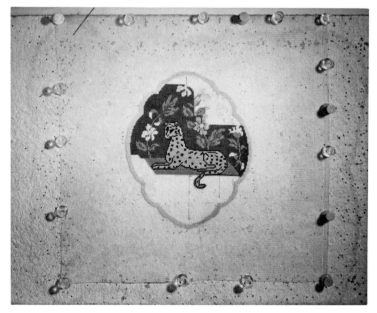

Finished rug being blocked, showing how staples hold it taut.

Finishing the Edges

Petit point pieces worked on fine silk gauze are finished by gluing or stitching the edge under. Rugs on cotton canvas are finished by binding the edge or sewing the ends back in.

For sewing, turn the edges under so that no gauze shows beyond the stitching, and cut excess material from under the corners so that they lay as flat as possible. Cut the gauze no wider than ¼" from the petit point; it is sometimes easier to do this after the sewing has been completed. Sew with small stitches and be careful not to go through to the front of the work.

When gluing an edge, be sure to use a fabric glue, such as Velverette, that will not bleed through to the surface of the piece. Gluing makes a rather stiff edge and can be helpful in keeping things like a bellpull flat. Lay the piece on a sheet of waxed paper and dry it between two heavy books.

To give rugs a nice thin edge, use this procedure. Unravel the canvas on all four sides back to the stitching. Don't be nervous—it won't fall apart in your lap. Now you should have a fringe all around the 2" of unraveled margin. Take a #22 tapestry needle and thread it with two strands of the fringe. Run the needle under the stitches on the back of the rug, at a right angle to the edge, for ½". Cut the ends off close to the work. We usually start working in the center of a side and go toward the corners. This will not work on interlocked canvas because it will not unravel easily. For that use sewing, gluing, or binding.

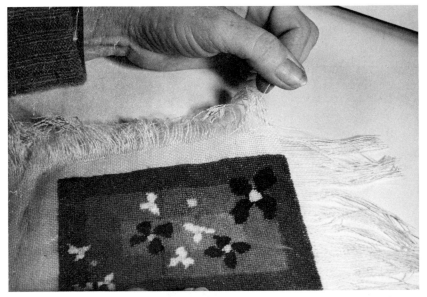

Unraveling the edge of a finished rug in preparation for the final finishing.

Stitching unraveled threads into underside of rug.

Binding

There is a stitch that can be used for binding edges with thread. It makes the edge a bit thicker but looks very neat. Fold the canvas under so that one mesh, two threads, lie on top of the edge. Hold the right side of the piece toward you and work from left to right. Follow the diagram for placing the stitches. This is basically a back-and-forth overcast stitch. The excess canvas may be cut off close to the work upon completion of the edge.

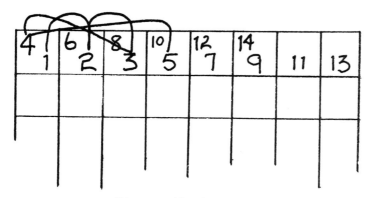

Diagram of binding stitch.

PETIT POINT APPLIED TO FURNITURE

When needlework has to be applied to a piece of furniture as shown on the wing chair, run a line of diluted white glue along the edge of the last row of stitching to keep the threads from raveling when excess gauze is cut away. With a fine brush, run a line of glue on the chair edge where the piece is to be glued. Press very firmly into position on all edges and allow to dry. Cut away excess gauze with very sharp, fine scissors close to the chair edge. When the chair has thoroughly dried, apply braid to cover the seams by applying a thin line of undiluted white glue. Work ½" at a time, pressing braid firmly in place. Keep a damp cloth at hand to keep your fingers free of glue. Cording may also be used as a trim.

Wing chair partially upholstered.

Run a line of glue along the finished
edge of the petit point.

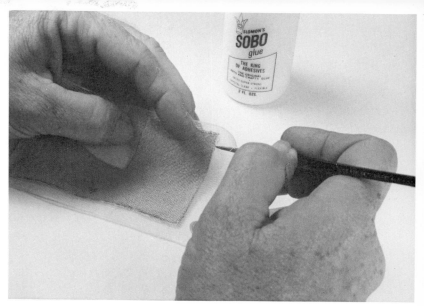

Apply glue to the furniture.

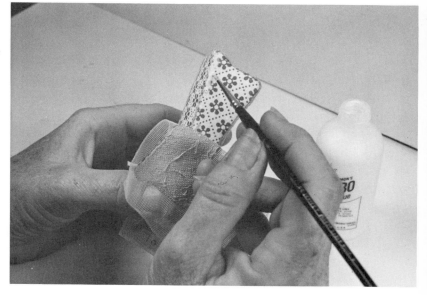

Press panel into position over glue.

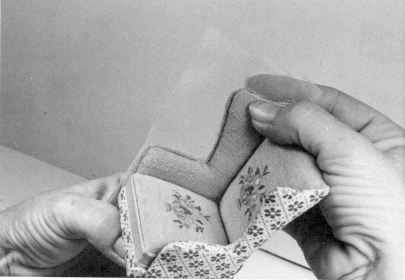

Cut away excess silk gauze.

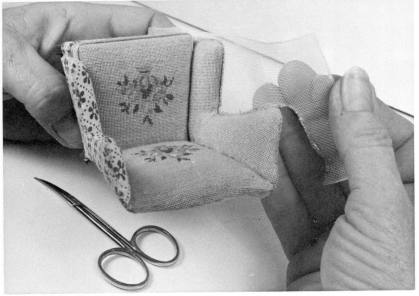

Apply braid to cover seams.

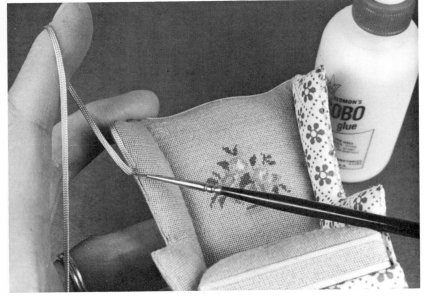

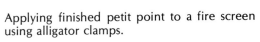

Applying finished petit point to a fire screen using alligator clamps.

MAKING CORDING AND FRINGE

To make cording, use a thread of DMC embroidery floss. Anchor one end securely with a clamp, then twist the thread, rolling it between your fingers. Keep twisting until the thread is very tight. Place your finger on the center of the thread and bring the anchored end and the free end together. The piece will twist back upon itself forming a cord. Knot the ends together.

Making a simple cording using DMC embroidery floss.

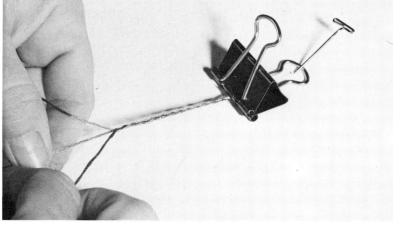

To make cording, anchor end of embroidery floss firmly and twist between your fingers.

When floss is twisted tight, let it twist back on itself and knot ends together.

If you wish, you may put fringe on your rug, although this is not necessary. Fringe on Oriental rugs is the warp left long. This does not look well when using petit point canvas or gauze. You must apply fringe after the rug is blocked and the edges finished.

Use ½ strand (3 threads) of DMC embroidery floss in ecru and a very small crochet hook. Cut the threads into 3" lengths. Hold the rug with the back toward you and insert the hook. Catch the embroidery floss in the center and pull it through to make a loop. Take the loose ends and pull them through the loop. Yank on the ends to tighten the fringe. Fringe is never put on all four sides of a rug, just the ends. When you have finished applying the fringe, take sharp scissors and cut it off evenly; do not leave it too long or it will be out of proportion to the rug.

Insert crochet hook from back to front of rug, catching thread at center.

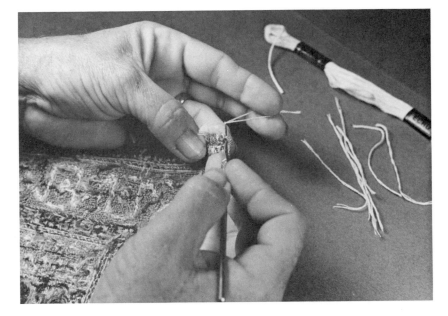

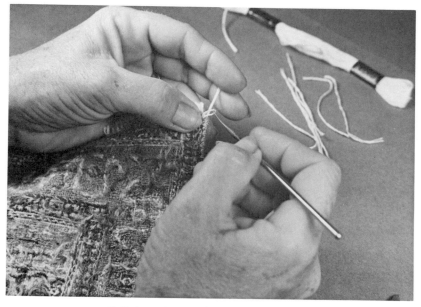

Pull thread toward you to form a loop.

Pull ends through the loop and tighten.

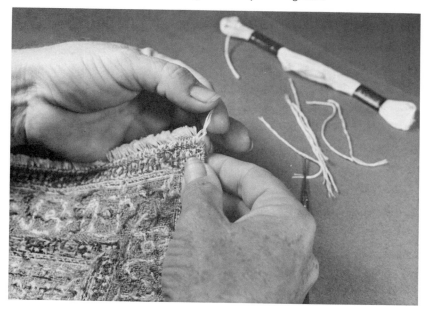

COMPLETED RUGS AND SMALL PIECES

Two rugs made by Judith Ohanian. Top rug is a Greek key design, the bottom rug is a Sarouk design. Courtesy, Judith Ohanian. Photograph by Ralph Feldman.

Aubusson rug. Collection of Elizabeth Ellis. Designed and made by Jean Jessop.

Chinese rug. Made by Barbara Bergraph. Designed by E. Art Kuns. Kit available from Boutique Margot.

Two-tone Bargello rug. Made by Meg Brown. Courtesy, Meg Brown.

Greek Key Oriental and a sailing ship 1⅞″ by 2¾″. Made by Meg Brown. Courtesy, Meg Brown.

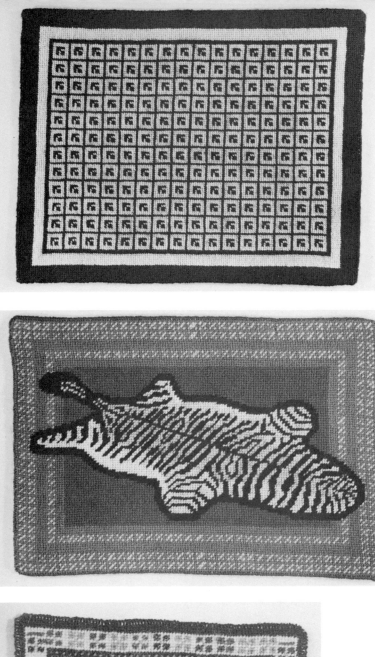

Flower rug. Designed and made by Jane Sikora. From Calico Miniatures. Courtesy, Calico Miniatures.

Zebra rug. Designed and made by Jane Sikora, from Calico Miniatures. Courtesy, Calico Miniatures.

Caucasian rug.

Chinese rug. Collection of Elizabeth Ellis. Designed and made by Jean Jessop.

Gobelin stitch rug. Designed and made by Jean Jessop.

A Tabriz, afghan, and prayer rug, all made by Judith Ohanian. Courtesy, Judith Ohanian. Photograph by Ralph Feldman.

Chinese rug 5½" by 7¼". Made by Gloria B. Richardson. Courtesy, Gloria B. Richardson.

Three Persian rugs. Collection of Elizabeth Ellis. Designed and made by Jean Jessop.

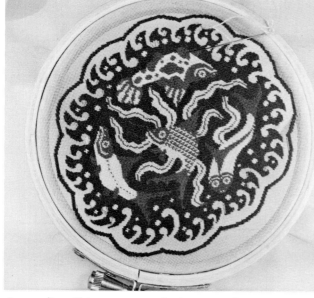

A very fine Chinese rug worked on #48 silk gauze, using a hoop. Made by Barbara Bergrath, from a design by Maggie Lane from her book CHINESE RUGS DESIGNED FOR NEEDLEPOINT, published by Charles Scribner's Sons.

Petit point rug. Made by Sally Brackett.

Animal rug. Designed and made by Julie Pitney, using DMC embroidery floss.

Samarkand rug. Collection of Virginia Merrill. Designed and made by Jean Jessop.

Persian prayer rug. Collection of Virginia Merrill. Designed and made by Jean Jessop.

Persian rug.

English flowered rug. Designed and made by Jean Jessop.

Embroidered bed set and coordinated needlework. Available in kit form from Create Your Own, Inc. Courtesy, Create Your Own.

A variety of petit point items. Available in kit form from Create Your Own, Inc. Courtesy, Create Your Own.

Petit point rug and chair seats. Available in kits from Create Your Own, Inc. Courtesy, Create Your Own.

116

This floral design that was previously charted is used as a picture.

A very fine petit point piece. Made by Mitzi Van
Horn to be mounted on a fire screen.

Sampler worked on #38 silk gauze is 2" x 3" using
1 thread of DMC embroidery floss. Designed
and made by Virginia Merrill.

A beautifully worked sampler on fine silk gauze. Made
by Martha Farnsworth. Collection of Virginia Merrill.

Swan tapestry, 3″ x 5″ on #38 gauze with cotton, silk, and g[...] threads. Designed and made [...] Jean Jessop.

Petit point worked on an eve[...] weave fabric, thus eliminating [...] need to fill in a background. Ma[...] by Marian K. Stannard.

Elephant design on even-weave fabric. Made by Marian K. Stannard.

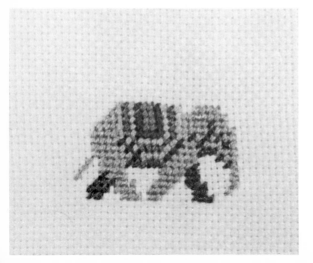

Camel design on even-weave fabric in petit point. Made by Marian K. Stannard.

Exquisitely dressed bride by Susan Sirkis.

Fire screen worked on #48 silk gauze by Virginia Merrill.

sop's prayer rug, enhanced by a violin and cello made by W
racy.

Bunny motif in petit point made by Virginia
Merrill on a footstool.

Victorian chair with Barge[l]
Susan Richardson.

Embroidered wall hanging
by Jean Jessop.

Petit point straps on lugga[ge]
rack by Jean Jessop, embroid[ered]
on frame and frame made [by]
Virginia Merrill.

Petit point rug by Jean Jessop.

Safari room with leopard rug by Virginia Merrill. Telescope and firearms by Jim Holmes.

A delicately created doll by Susan Sirkis.

Cherry Lady by Susan Sirkis.

Tiger rug in petit point by Virginia Merrill.

Two wing chairs. Bargello on left by Jean Jessop, chair on the right by Virginia Merrill, unfinished to show the possibility of covering an already completed chair.

Crocheted baby set by Patty Highfill. Collection: Jacqueline Andrews.

Crocheted bed cover by Ruth Black. Collection: Jacqueline Andrews.

Transylvania church carpet, 18th-century Turkish design, by Barbara Cosgrove of Needleworks in Miniature.

Jean Jessop's petit point animal rug.

Backgammon Board 2″x2¾″ by Susan Richardson.

Chinese rug by Virginia Merrill, from a very early Chinese rug design. Rugs of this type were made in various ground colors, blue being the most common, but rose and yellow and beige were also used extensively.

Petit point designs on even-weave fabric used for greeting cards. Made by Marian K. Stannard.

Austrian petit point portrait 3⅝" x 4⅞". From the collection of Mr. & Mrs. Harold R. Towers. Courtesy, Mr. & Mrs. Harold R. Towers.

Petit point picture of a nude, from Austria, 2½" x 3". Collection of Mr. & Mrs. Harold R. Towers. Courtesy, Mr. & Mrs. Harold R. Towers.

Petit point pastoral scene 3¼" x 4⅞". Collection of Mr. &
Mrs. Harold R. Towers. Courtesy, Mr. & Mrs. Harold R.
Towers.

Floral spray design on even-weave fabric. Made by Marian K. Stannard.

120

PETIT POINT APPLIED TO FURNITURE

Settee upholstered with a piece of antique petit point. Made by Eugene Kupjack.

Stool and corner chair worked on #38 silk gauze. Designed and made by Virginia Merrill.

Bed steps. Available from Paige Thornton.

Petit point chair seats. Available from Create Your Own, Inc. Courtesy, Create Your Own.

Two pole screens worked on silk gauze. Left: Designed and made by Susan Richardson. Right: Designed and made by Virginia Merrill.

Petit point stool and chair seat. Made by Martha Dinkel of The Mouse Hole.

Checkerboard chair seat and yarn
caddy. Made by Cookie Ziemba.

French gilt settee and chairs wit[h]
petit point upholstery. Collection [of]
Jean Jessop.

Bed steps with embroidered desig[n]
and fire screen worked in peti[t]
point. Made by Cookie Ziemba.

Settee seat made from an antiqu[e]
petit point handbag. Collection o[f]
Susan Richardson.

Bargello-covered stool. Made by Martha Dinkel of
The Mouse Hole.

Needle point frame with petit point worked on #40 silk gauze, corner chair
with checkerboard design on #40 silk, and footstool worked on #58 silk gauze.
Made by Cookie Ziemba.

PETIT POINT APPLIED TO PILLOWS

Five petit point pillows. Designed and made by Barbara Bergrath.

A collection of petit point pillows, tatted doilies, and a braided rug. Made by Mary Frances Olson. Courtesy, Mary Frances Olson.

Petit point pillows with geometric designs. Designed and made by Elizabeth Scull.

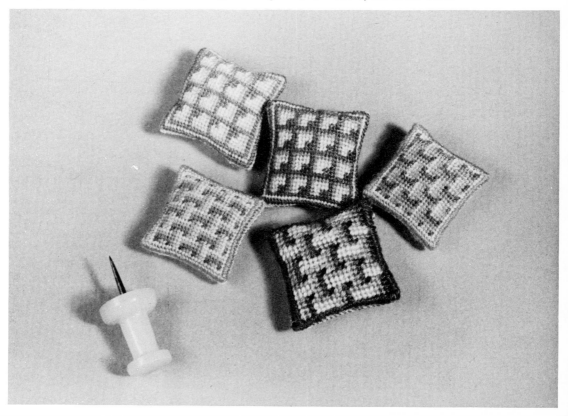

A fine piece designed and made by Susan Richardson that can be used as a cover for a chair seat, stool, or pillow.

3

OTHER NEEDLEWORK TECHNIQUES

EMBROIDERY AND CROSS-STITCH
Basic Working Materials

You will need skeins or spools of silk, cotton, or rayon thread, #10 crewel needles, embroidery hoop, small, sharp scissors, thimble, magnifying equipment, transfer patterns, tracing paper, architects' linen, dressmakers' carbon paper, graphite paper, Wallace Hi-Speed extra-fine repro #113 black pencil or an indelible ball-point pen.

An assortment of embroidery materials. Silk thread, needles, iron-on transfer patterns, scissors, marking pen, and a magnifying glass with lights.

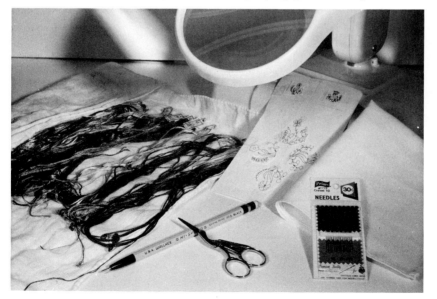

Background Material

The fabric for background must be a fine preshrunk material such as handkerchief linen or an even-weave cotton or polyester.

Threads

Your choice of thread depends on the finished effect you wish to achieve. Silk and rayon thread is more difficult to work and creates a brighter sheen to your design. Cotton thread, such as DMC (mouline special) will give a softer, duller effect. Using a single thread is recommended for a finer finish to your work.

Needles

For all miniature embroidery and cross-stitch, #10 crewel needles are used. They are shorter and have a larger eye than regular embroidery needles.

The Hoop

The hoop is an important vehicle in creating fine embroidery. It holds the material taut, thus eliminating any irregularity in your work, and keeps the stitches neat and even. Delicate fabric may be distorted and stretched by the hoop's rim. This can be eliminated by placing a piece of fabric, or an old linen handkerchief, with a 2″ x 3″

An extra piece of fabric is placed over the work to keep it clean.

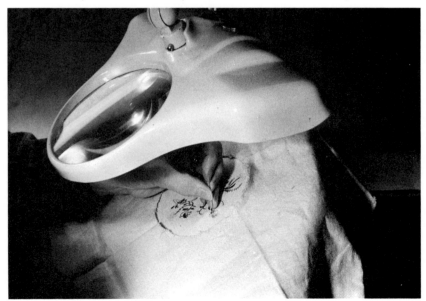

hole cut out of the center, over your work and clamped in the hoop. This will also keep your embroidery clean.

Transferring the Design

Small transfer patterns are readily available commercially and are simply ironed onto your background material according to the directions on the package.

Another method is to transfer your own or a printed design by laying a piece of architects' linen or tracing paper over the design and tracing the outline in pencil. Then get your fabric, take a piece of dressmakers' carbon or graphite paper, shiny side down, design on top, secure in place at the very outer edge with pushpins, and trace around the design with a hard pencil, applying pressure to ensure a good, clear transfer. Remove paper and carbon and your piece is ready to mount in a hoop and be stitched.

Transfers arranged on fabric, held in place with Scotch tape, and ready to be ironed on.

Working the stitches with silk embroidery thread.

The very fine embroidered bed-spread completed. Designed and made by Mary Fry.

Transfer designs, used for embroidered pictures. Made by Mary Fry.

The Stitches

With the development of some 350 related stitches, dating back to Abraham and Biblical times and continuing as part of the cultural development of every nation, we have diagramed a few basic stitches for your use in creating your own needlework.

Stem stitch

Working from left to right, come up at 1, down at 2, up at 3, down at 4, up at 2, in the same hole as was worked previously, always keeping the thread on the same side of the needle, in this case at the bottom. The stem stitch is a good outline stitch.

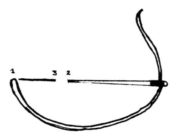

Stem stitch diagram.

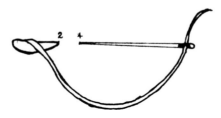

Satin stitch

Working from bottom to top, come up at 1, down at 2, keeping the stitches close and even and preserving a neat firm edge.

Satin stitch diagram.
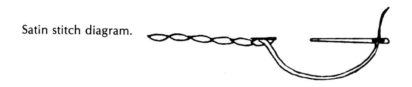

Slanted satin stitch

Work as for satin stitch, slanting the stitches to the shape required.

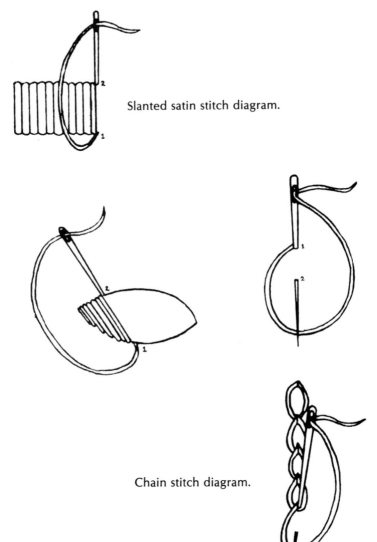

Slanted satin stitch diagram.

Chain stitch diagram.

Chain stitch

Starting at 1, bring needle up through fabric, forming a loop. Go down again at 1 in the same hole, holding loop down with the thumb. Bring needle up at 2 holding the needle on top of thread at bottom of loop. Repeat same procedure, keeping loops uniform.

Buttonhole stitch

Working from left to right, bring needle up at 1, down at 2, up at 3, passing thread under the needle. Continue steps 2 and 3 until completed. This stitch may also be worked closely together to form a more padded effect.

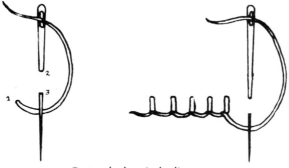

Buttonhole stitch diagram.

Cross-stitch

Starting at the right and working left, bring the needle up at 1, down at 2, up at 3, down at 4, and so on across row to be worked. This forms the first half of each cross. Working from left to right, come up at a, down at b, up at c, down at d, until all the crosses are completed. Cross-stitches must be worked on a fabric of which the threads may be counted and are an even weave.

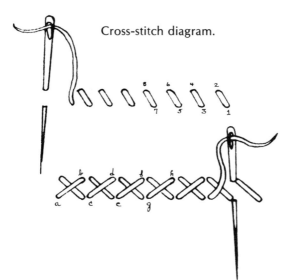

Cross-stitch diagram.

Backstitch

Working from right to left, come up at 1, back down at 2, up again at 3, back down at 4, up at 5, back down at 6, and so on until the design is completed.

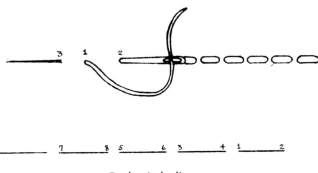

Back stitch diagram.

Coral stitch

Working from right to left, come up at 1, laying thread in the direction of the line of work, holding thread down with left thumb. Needle then enters in at 2 and up at 3, over top of bottom loop of thread, forming a series of knots at right angles to the line of work. The knots may be spaced according to the desired effect.

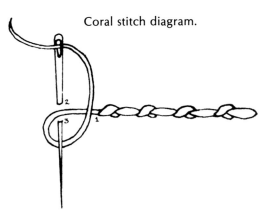

Coral stitch diagram.

Finishing

Because of the delicate nature of the fabric required for miniature embroidery, when the work is completed, it should be handled with great care. If the piece is soiled from handling, it should be dipped in a solution of Ivory Flakes dissolved in lukewarm water. Squeeze gently, do not rub, rinse thoroughly, and lay on a towel to dry. Press very gently with a warm iron, face down on a soft towel.

Your piece is now ready for use as a framed picture, bedspread, drapery, pillow, sampler, or whatever use you have predetermined.

A Gallery of Examples

Cross-stitch sampler. Made by Anne Gi Conte.

Embroidered flower motif, a good design for a bedspread.

137

Larger-size antique sampler on even-weave fabric. Many of our designs today are taken from old samplers such as this.

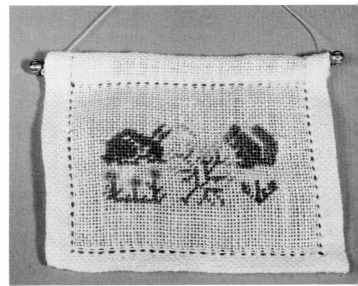

Wall hanging worked on even-weave linen, #32 mesh, in cross stitch, with DMC embroidery floss. Made by Julie Pitney.

Two cross-stitch samplers. Made by Anne Gi Conte.

...roidered bed cover and va-... Available in kit form from ...te Your Own, Inc. Courtesy, ...te Your Own.

...s-stitch bed cover. Available in ...orm from Create Your Own,

...roidered bed cover and pillow. ...gned and made by Virginia ...rill.

An Elizabethan black and gold design on Hardanger fabric, using 1 thread of DMC embroidery floss and Talon gold thread. Designed and made by Jeanne Knoop.

An Elizabethan black and gold picture. Designed and r by Jeanne Knoop.

Embroidered draperies, chair, and sofa. Available from Create Your Own, Inc., in kits. Courtesy, Create Your Own.

140

BRAIDED RUGS

From the time the Pilgrims used cornhusks to make their floor coverings to the Colonists who later began weaving fabric for clothing, rags and scraps and worn clothing were saved, cut into strips, and rolled into balls for making rugs. Their popularity endured because of the availability of material, their attractive color tones, designs, and durability. Their shapes were varied, from round to oval, oblong or square.

The miniature rug, however, is not made from fabric scraps but from an appropriate ply yarn to keep the rug thin and flat. In miniature, a rug made from fabrics would be much too thick and heavy.

Materials

The basic materials for a braided rug are a 4-ply knitting worsted for a 1" to the foot scale, or 3 ply for ½" to the foot scale, a clamp for anchoring ends of yarn while braiding, needle, sewing thread, scissors, and a thimble.

How to Determine Size

If, for example, you want to make a 5" x 7" oval rug, the center core should be 2" long. To find the proper length for the center core, subtract the width of the finished size from the length. For example, with a 5" x 7" rug, subtract 5" from 7", which equals a 2" core. A 4" x 8" would equal a 4" core.

Choosing the Colors

The color scheme should be made up of 3 color groups:
Neutral colors—gray, beige, off-white.
Vivid colors—red, green, orange, yellow, and navy.
Dark colors—brown, black, navy.

Start with the neutral tones and work out with the vivid and darker tones. Always finish the last border with the dark colors. This frames the rug and gives a more balanced effect.

How to Braid

Start by tying 3 strands of knitting worsted together, and clamp tied ends to a board to secure for braiding. Lift right strand over center strand and lay it down. Lift left strand over right strand, which became center. Then lift right over center and continue this process of right over left and left over right until the strands are fully braided. Keep the tension even throughout the braiding. Form the lengths of braid into desired shape, either round or oval, oblong or square, stitching each row carefully together on the underside of rug. Ease around curves so that rug will not "turtle" up in the center. Hold rug flat while stitching. When joining or butting one end of a braid to another, simply use a small overcast stitch on underside of rug.

Tie the ends of 3 strands of 4-ply knitting worsted together.

Clamp ends. Lift right strand over center strand and lay it down.

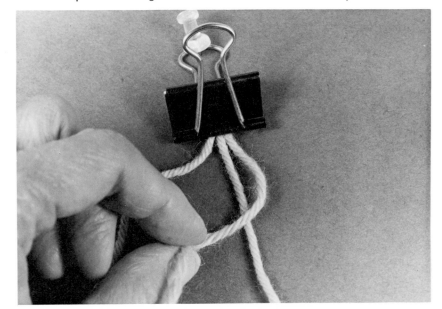

left strand over right strand, ch becomes center.

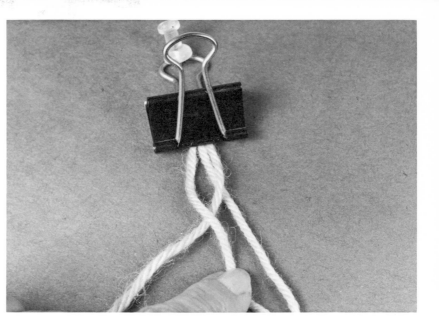

n lift right over center strand. tinue this process of left over t and right over left.

Keep tension even.

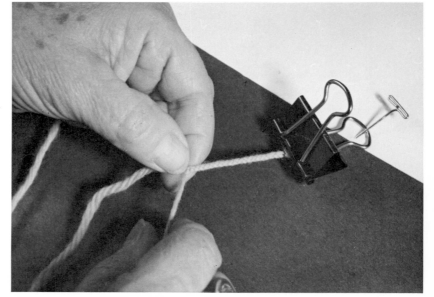

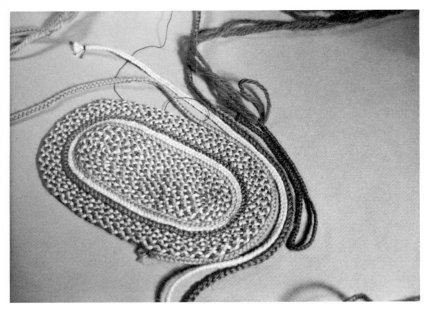

Form lengths of braid into desire[d] shape, either round or oval, stitch[ing] each row carefully togethe[r] Ease around curves so that the ru[g] will not "turtle" up.

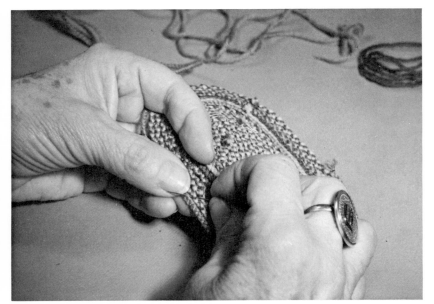

Hold rug flat while stitching.

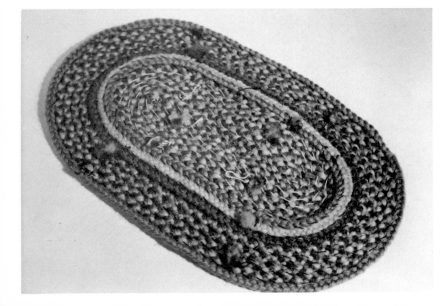

Underside of completed rug sho[w] ing stitching pattern. This rug w[as] made by Carol Dinkel.

Two exceptionally nice rugs. Made by Carol Dinkel.

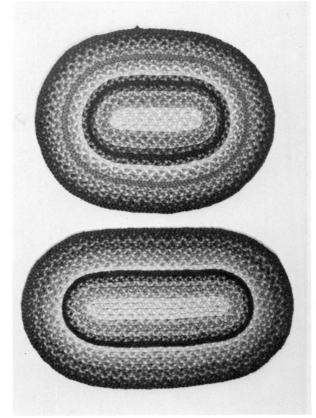

Braided rug 9″ x 11″. Made by Gloria B. Richardson. Courtesy, Gloria B. Richardson.

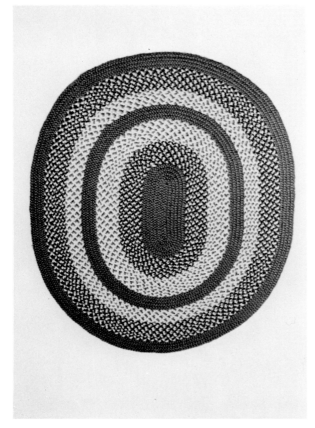

Two Shaker rugs 4″ in diameter. Made by Gloria B. Richardson. Courtesy, Gloria B. Richardson.

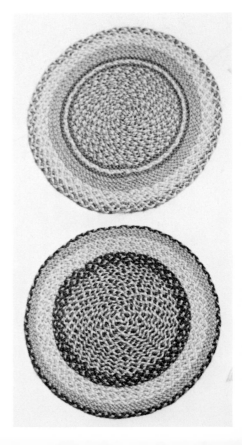

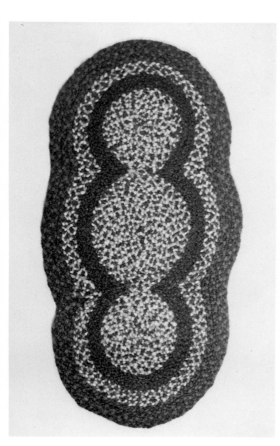

An unusually shaped braided rug. Made by Rita Reher.

Crocheted afghan and braided rug. Made by Rita Reher.

HOOKED RUGS

Hooked rugs are an American invention, dating from Colonial times. Today there is a revival of the art.

For miniature rugs you should use wool; one thread of Persian needlepoint wool works well, or knitted worsted can be used. The backing is an even-weave material of a fairly tight weave such as Hardanger cloth.

The miniature hooker is available by mail order from our Sources of Supply list at the back of the book. The directions on the package must be followed carefully. Try a practice piece first. Be sure to keep the end of the wool, coming out of the top of the hooker, completely free; if you don't, you are apt to pull out the loops you have worked. You will work with the back side toward you. Try to make the loops close enough so that the backing doesn't show but not so close that the piece humps up. This is where practice will help. The loops will lock themselves in place.

Draw the design for your rug directly on the material with an indelible marker. The simple traditional designs are the most effective. There are many books in the library about early American rooms and they are full of ideas for hooked rugs. After you draw

Working with a miniature rug hooker, using 1 strand of Persian wool on an even-weave fabric, creates a very nice small hooked rug. Hooker available from Doreen Sinnett Designs.

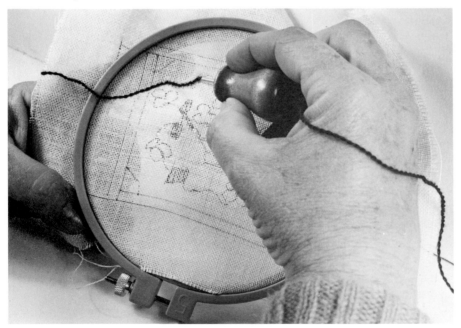

your design on the material, put it in an embroidery hoop and make sure that the material is very taut. Outline the design with the wool first, then fill in. Do the background last.

When the hooking is completed, turn a hem under and stitch down.

Since the rugs are thick, do not plan to use them in a place where it will be necessary to put furniture on them, particularly one leg of a chair, or they will make the furniture tilt. They are most useful in a hall, beside a bed, or in the middle of a room.

A completed hooked rug.

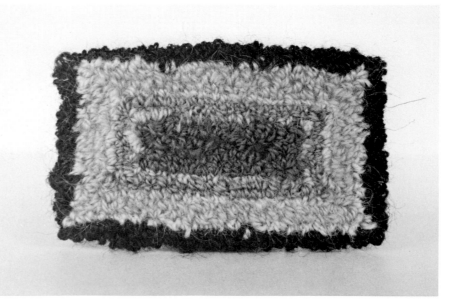

THE FRENCH KNOTTED RUG

The knotted rug produces a texture very much like a hooked rug. The French knot is made by bringing the thread up from the back of the material, taking one turn of the thread around the needle, pulling tight, then inserting the needle back next to the hole where the thread emerged.

The backing can be Belgian linen, Hardanger cloth, or a polyester of an even weave. The thread used on the rug pictured was three strands of DMC embroidery floss, with a #5 crewel needle.

As in the hooked rug, draw the design directly on the backing and fill in with French knots. An embroidery hoop is helpful in keeping the backing flat during the knotting.

When the rug is completed, turn the edges under and hem.

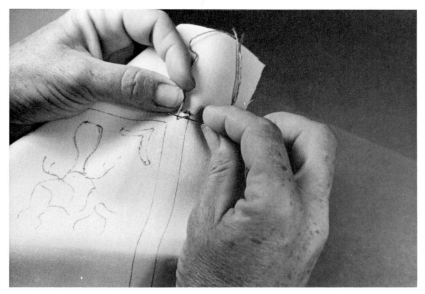

Wrap one turn around the needle.

Pull thread tight around needle, insert back into fabric.

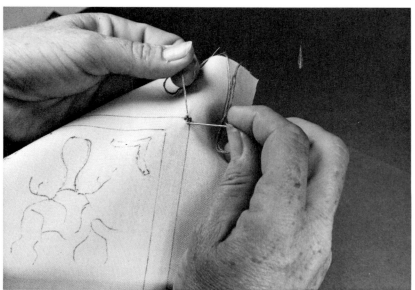

Detail of a finished rug.

The whole rug containing over 20,000 French knots, using 3 threads of DMC embroidery floss. Made by Meg Brown. Courtesy, Meg Brown.

A PATCHWORK QUILT

Patchwork is an old established American folk art that portrays American tradition and history.

Constructed of various shapes and sizes, the patches are arranged in a juxtaposition according to the quilter's plan and design. The patches are sewn together on the wrong side either by hand or machine, pressing seams open to keep piece flat and neat. The second layer consists of a piece of art foam or fine cotton batting to give a padded effect, and the third layer, which is the backing or lining, is held in place by tufting or tying the three layers together at specific intervals. When tufting or tying on the right side, the thread forms a pleasant, decorative effect.

When making a miniature quilt, the fabric is a matter of choice. However, these very small quilts require a delicate, thin fabric such as preshrunk cotton or linen, with a design that follows the proper scale of 1" to a foot. The fabric may also be of plain fabric arranged in a pleasing design of complementary colors. A color wheel is a very helpful device in your choice of coordinated colors and careful color placement.

Quilting supplies

DMC embroidery floss—for tufting or tying
Fine cotton or linen fabric—for patch pieces and backing
Art Foam or thin cotton batting ⅛" thick—for padding
Scissors
#10 crewel needles

Quilting supplies.

Procedure for assembling quilt

Cut out 1" squares and lay them out in the order that they are to be sewn together. Pin in place and sew units together with ⅛" seams. Press seams flat. Cut out backing piece 1" larger than patchwork piece. Cover backing with a piece of art foam that has been cut the same size as patchwork rectangle. Place quilted piece on top of art foam, thus creating 3 layers. Fold extended edge of backing ½" down, mitering all four corners. Make a second fold over edge of patchwork surface. Pin in place. You may also baste to keep layers from shifting. Tie the intersecting corners of each square to secure the 3 layers, and transform the patchwork into a 3-dimensional surface. The backing edges are also tied with stitches matching those in the squares.

Press the border edge with care, but not the patchwork. This should remain puffy.

Back of quilt after sewing squares together.

The three layers, patchwork, Art Foam, and backing.

Fold extended edge of backing ½″
down, mitering each corner.

Then make a second fold over top
edge of quilt.

Pin in place.

Tie intersecting corners of each
square to secure three layers.

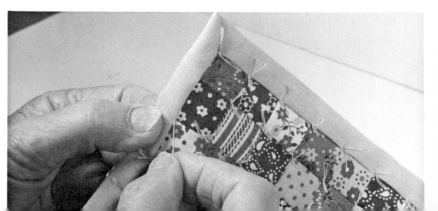

Tie border edges with stitches matching those in the squares.

Finished patchwork quilt. Made by Susan Richardson.

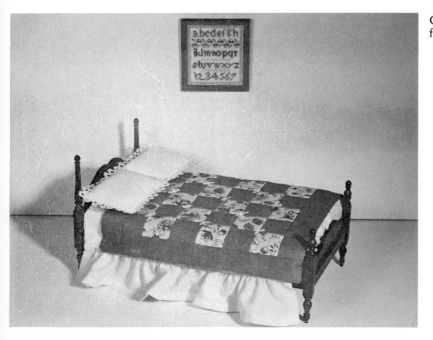

Quilt and sampler available in kit form from June Dole.

Dressed doll. Made by Virginia Merrill.

DRESSING A DOLL

Miniature dolls to be used in dollhouse settings have grown in popularity with the great surge in miniature making and collecting. Dolls have been made and used over the past centuries, but today the miniature doll ½" to about 7½" has become more popular with collectors than ever before.

Designers and makers of these small dolls find the demand greater than their ability to produce them, as is true with Margaret Finch, Carol Nordell, Irma Park, and Susan Sirkis to name a few. Their expert craftsmanship and precise duplication of fashions have made their dolls collector's items.

A very important fashion era was a period from the year 1830 through the 1870s, when Mr. Louis A. Godey's *Lady's Book* set a fashion pattern for the nineteenth century. His ladies were dressed in fabrics of silk, satin, organdy, and taffeta, obscuring frilly pantalets, and layered petticoats. Skirts with flounces and ruffles, bedecked with ribbon and lace, added charm and elegance to the gowns of this period. Bodices were set off with puffed, bell-shaped, or leg-of-mutton sleeves. Wasp waists gave shape to a truly lovely costume.

Bonnets adorned with feathers and bows, hoods for winter wear, caps or fauchons for morning habits (also referred to as handkerchief caps) were decorated with lace and embroidery.

Jackets, mantles, and shawls were worn over a fitted bodice to complete the outfit.

The challenge of keeping in scale the components of dressing a small doll is of considerable importance. Fabrics must be delicate and thin. The lace and ribbon should be the very finest, and the stitches that bind them together supersmall. Oftentimes, white glue is used to secure a bodice or sleeve in place rather than risking a too-large stitch from showing. As a result, these dolls are permanently dressed.

Fashion accessories in the late nineteenth century became numerous and elaborate. No grande toilette was complete without a lovely parasol, fan, purse, and slippers. And, of course, gloves were considered a touch of elegance. So please enter into our small world of fashion and dress a doll. These patterns and directions are for a 6½″ doll.

Cut pantalets from pattern #1, using white cotton fabric. Turn a ⅛″ hem at the bottom and sew 3 rows of lace across the edge of each piece. Sew front and back seams, press seams open. Stitch inside leg seams. Sew a machine basting around the waist and pull thread to fit doll's waist, secure thread. Cut white cotton fabric for the petticoat 12″ long and 2¼″ deep. Sew back seam to within 1″ of waistline. Turn ⅛″ hem at bottom of petticoat and add rows of lace to reach ankle. Sew a machine-basting stitch at waistline and pull thread to fit doll's waist, secure thread.

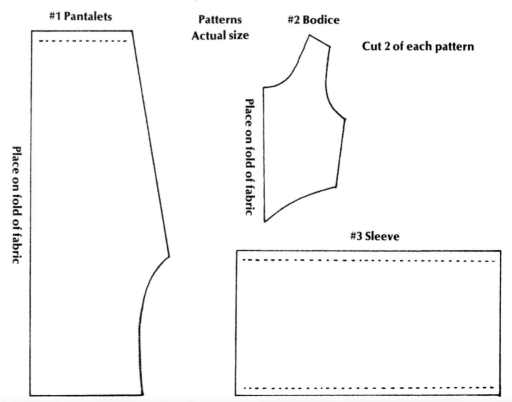

#1 Pantalets

Patterns
Actual size

#2 Bodice

Cut 2 of each pattern

Place on fold of fabric

Place on fold of fabric

Place on fold of fabric

#3 Sleeve

Stitched front seam of pantalet.

Leg seams after stitching and pressing.

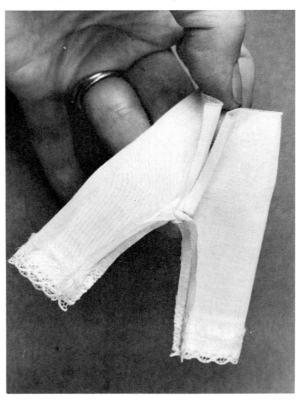

Sew a drawstring around waist and pull to fit waist, secure. Thread.

Fitting petticoat to doll, pulling drawstring to waist size.

Cut dress skirt fabric 12" long and 4" deep, if it is to be hemmed; 3½" deep, if no hem is needed. Stitch back seam to within 1" of waist. Press seam open. Sew machine-basting stitches from back seam of waist to within 1" of center front on each side. This creates a smooth effect across front of skirt and fullness from sides to back. Cut 2 bodice pieces from pattern #2. Sew or glue in place directly onto body of doll, turning under edges where necessary. Trim neck with lace ruffle. Cut sleeves from pattern #3. Sew machine-basting stitch at top and bottom edges as indicated on pattern by dotted lines. Sew or glue underarm seam. Pull gathering threads while fitting to doll's arms. Sleeves may be stitched or glued into place at armhole.

Fitting skirt to doll over petticoat.

Sleeve piece with two rows of gathering.

Pulling two rows of gathering.

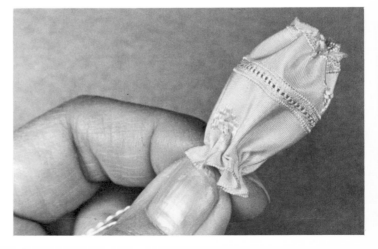

For the shirred bonnet, using same fabric as the dress, cut a piece 9½" long by 2¼" wide. Turn a ¼" hem at one long edge and sew or glue into place. Sew machine-basting row of stitches at the hemmed edge ⅝" from edge. Sew a machine-basting row of stitches ⅛" from edge of opposite long edge and pull gathering thread as tightly as possible, secure thread. Pin to board to hold firmly in place while pulling second row of gathering threads. Pull gathers just enough to fit head of doll, secure thread.

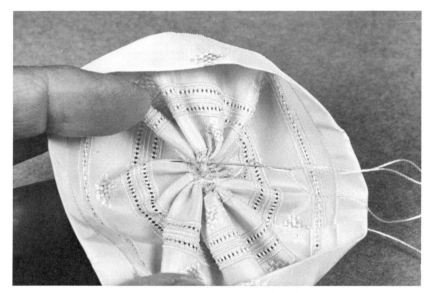

Bonnet. Pulling center row of gathers.

Pulling outside row of gathers.

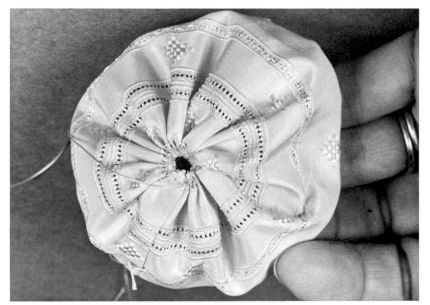

Bonnet after two rows have been gathered and secured by tying threads.

Another type of handmade bonnet. Made by The Wee Hatter.

MAKING A PARASOL

What could complete an outfit for a fashion doll more than a lovely parasol?

The basic materials needed are a 4" embroidery hoop, white glue, paint, a compass, alligator clamps (available at Electronic Supply Stores) or hairclips, very thin fabric, lace, or other trimming, scissors, and a paper parasol.

The frame is made from a paper parasol, readily found in a hobby, party, or craft shop. There are two sizes; use the one that measures 3¾" from top to bottom. The body may be made of lace, silk, nylon, or any delicate thin fabric, and is usually trimmed with lace.

The first step is to measure, with a compass, from the center top to the tip of a rib, with the parasol in open position, to determine the size of the fabric circle. Stretch the fabric onto the hoop, keeping it taut. Find the center and draw a circle with the compass. Remove fabric from the hoop and cut a small ¼" hole in the center, to accommodate the top of the parasol. Cut the outside circle on the pencil line.

The paper is very carefully cut from between each rib to eliminate the colored paper. The ribs are painted with the same color as the fabric that is used, then allowed to dry.

Put a small amount of white glue on each rib and place fabric circle over top of ribs with parasol in open position. Trim edge with lace edging or an appropriate decorative braid.

Glue a small gold bead on bottom of shaft and trim with two small tassels (directions for same on page 77).

Parasol.

Supplies for making a parasol.

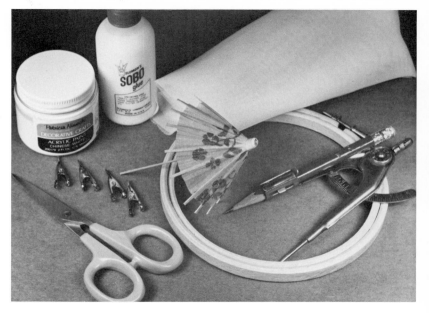

Measuring with a compass to determine fabric size.

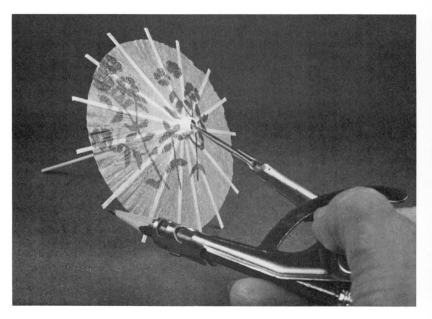

Fabric stretched on an embroidery hoop for drawing circle.

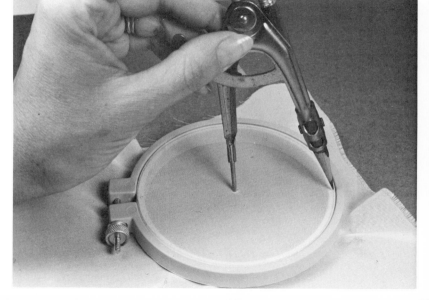

Paper being cut from between rib
of parasol.

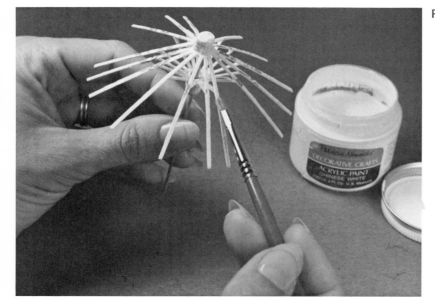

Painting each rib with acrylic pain

After applying white glue, plac
fabric on ribs and smooth down.

ter gluing fabric in place, as seen
m underneath.

m bottom edge with lace using
ite glue, and clamp with alligator
mps.

MAKING A PAIR OF LADIES' SLIPPERS

Many miniature accessories from a variety of materials are available from shops and individual craftsmen throughout the country. The photograph showing slippers, purse, and gloves are the creation of Pat Wyeth. Pat demonstrates in a photographic series the steps in making a pair of ladies' kid slippers.

Materials:

Kid gloves—white and brown
Velverette glue
Cuticle scissors

165

Procedure

Cut pattern #1 from a piece of white kid. Make a small cut along dotted line for top of shoe opening. Glue back seams, bringing them together so that they butt against each other, but do not overlap. This forms shape of shoe. Paper inner sole #2 is glued into place at bottom of shoe to hold shape. Glue an oblong piece of brown kid, larger than sole, to shoe bottom, then cut around shoe shape with small cuticle scissors. After glue sets, bend toe of shoe upward to shape. Roll a piece of white kid ¼" into a tight cylinder to form the heel. Glue edge to hold the shape. Glue pompon, flower, or bow at the toe of shoe and glue heel to back sole of shoe.

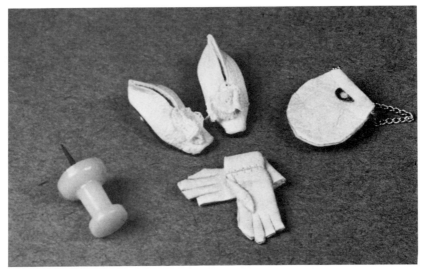

Accessories made from kid gloves. By Pat Wyeth of "On a Small Scale."

Supplies for making kid slippers.

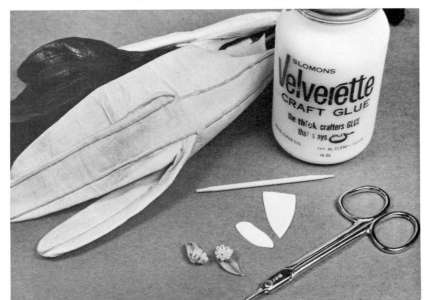

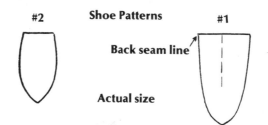

#2   Shoe Patterns   #1

Back seam line

Actual size

utting shoe shape from kid and
utting seams.

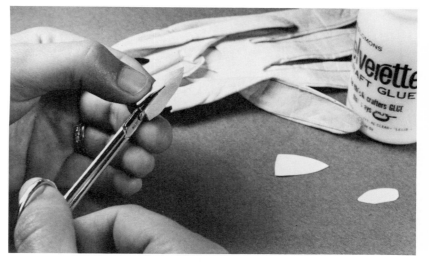

Gluing back seam.

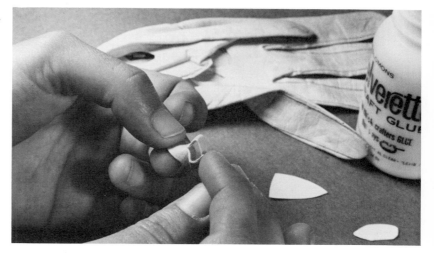

Inserting inner sole into shoe.

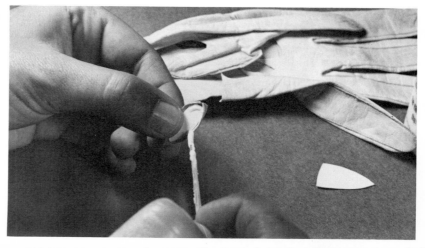

Glue shaped shoe to dark kid outer sole.

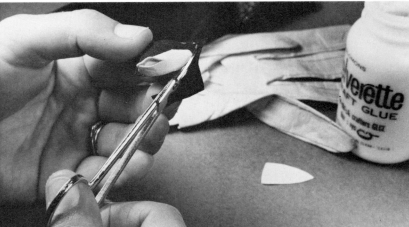

Cut sole to shape of shoe.

Bend toe of shoe upward to shape.

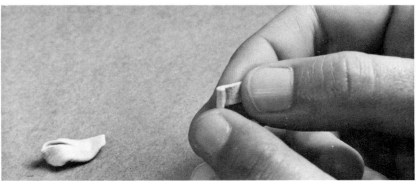

Roll a piece of kid ¼" x ½" to form heel gluing edge to hold.

Glue decoration to toe, and glue heel in place at the back of the sole.

EXAMPLES OF HAND-DRESSED DOLLS

Elaborately crocheted baby dress and bonnet. Doll and carriage from the Dollhouse Factory.

Antique bisque doll, hand-dressed in satin and lace. Collection of Susan Richardson.

dolls measuring 2". Made by ion Mullins.

Antique bisque dolls with crocheted dresses. Collection of Susan Richardson.

One-quarter-scale dolls with handmade clothes.

Lady Isabel De Cherlton, at the court of Edward III, 1350. This figure is carved of wood and painted with attention to anatomical detail. She wears the whitish makeup of the day. Created by Margaret Finch, N.I.D.A. Courtesy, Dearring-Tracy, Ltd. Photograph by Kenneth Clare.

Costumed doll. Made by Margaret Finch, N.I.D.A. Courtesy, Dearring-Tracy Ltd. Photograph by Kenneth Clare.

Exquisitely made and dressed doll by Susan Sirkis. Victorian crib, with hand-embroidered bed cover. Designed and made by Judee' A. Williamson of The Miniature Makers' Workshop.

Whimsical toys with hand-sewn costumes.

Marie Antoinette. Blue-and-white silk fabric mounted on a decoupage base. The fur on the dress is chiffon velvet. Designed and made by Susan Sirkis. Courtesy, The Wish Booklet.

A pretty girl. Ecru cotton fabric, with French blue ruching, lace trim. Bouquet made entirely of French knots. Designed and made by Susan Sirkis. Courtesy, The Wish Booklet.

The Princess de Lamballe. Pink and white silk costume. Designed and made by Susan Sirkis. Courtesy, The Wish Booklet.

group of beautifully dressed ladies. Designed and made by Susan Sirkis. Courtesy, The Wish Booklet.

Cherry lady 5½" tall. Designed and made by Susan Sirkis. Courtesy, The Wish Booklet. Photograph by Robert Sirkis.

Miss Gibson 1906. Yellow velvet and silk costume. Real kid gloves. Designed and made by Susan Sirkis. Courtesy, The Wish Booklet.

Winter costume, 1899. White wool, cream lace, and velvet "ermine." Designed and made by Susan Sirkis. Courtesy, The Wish Booklet.

173

Queen Elizabeth I. White satin and velvet, elaborately decorated. Designed and made by Susan Sirkis. Courtesy, The Wish Booklet.

Madam Baurgerit. White satin gown, beautifully sculptured to the body of the doll. Perky bows add a finishing touch. Designed and made by Susan Sirkis. Courtesy, The Wish Booklet.

Winter costume, 1533. Red velvet with simulated-velvet "ermine" trim. Designed and made by Susan Sirkis. Courtesy, The Wish Booklet.

DRESSING A BED

There are a great many miniature beds being made by today's craftsmen that are perfect reproductions of full-size beds. With a few basic materials and nimble fingers you can produce an exquisitely dressed bed. The American colonial-style bed, circa 1750–1780, has a relatively plain bed hanging and cover. The posts are simply turned, and the headboard has a slightly curved design. The fabric is an embroidered batiste that is draped in a very simple fashion, with a little fullness and no ruffles or frills.

The Sheraton-style fourposter here is copied from one made in New England, circa 1800. However, the early models had slimmer bedposts, which often were reeded and carved, and headboards that were higher and more shapely. In great contrast to the plain colonial-style bed, this one is dressed with a delicate cotton fabric, elaborately trimmed with frilly lace and ribbon.

The Hepplewhite bed features Swiss batiste hangings and pillows. A bonnet and dress are draped on the bed as though waiting for their owner to dress.

Beds were dressed with silk and satin and the finest laces and trimmings available. Sheets were as luxurious as their outer coverings, often made of satin with lace appliqué.

Hepplewhite-style furniture was popular in America circa 1785–1800. Pieces, usually rectilinear, were light and elegantly proportioned. Slim bedposts tapered upward and were often reeded or fluted.

Another bed that lends itself to draping is the alcove bed, so named because it is set into a recess in a wall. It is dressed on the front and sides, leaving the back bare to fit flat against the wall.

A cradle or baby's bed with high sides rests on short rockers, or is suspended between two vertical supports, enabling the cradle to be rocked back and forth. The Victorian cradle, dressed in satin and lace with a canopy of fine silk, is a typical example of many cradles of that time. The cradle eventually became obsolete in favor of the more practical crib.

American Colonial tester bed. Made by Donald Buttfield. Bed hangings and spread made by the Rumson Garden Club.

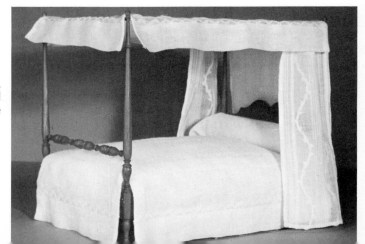

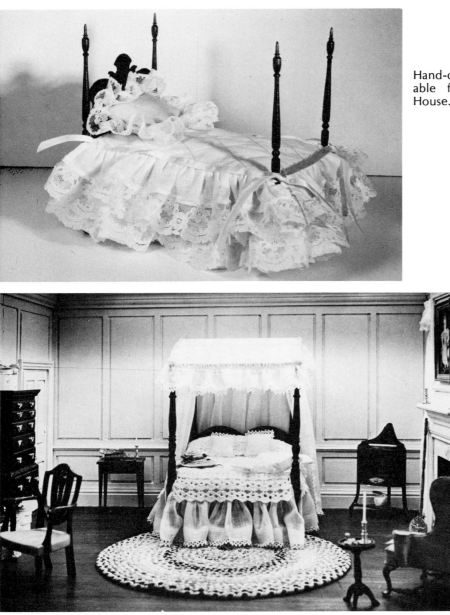

Hand-dressed Sheraton bed. Available from Lorrie Sweatt's Doll House.

Hepplewhite bedroom from Baby Wilton. Collection of Jacqueline Andrews. Courtesy, Jacqueline Andrews.

Exquisitely hand-dressed bed, Hepplewhite style. Designed and made by Judee' A. Williamson of The Miniature Makers' Workshop.

Hand-dressed alcove-style bed set. Available from Lorrie Sweatt's Doll House.

Victorian cradle with hand-sewn cover and drapery. Available from Lorrie Sweatt's Doll House.

Beautiful shadow box, encasing a Victorian cradle, draped with velvet and lace. Designed and made by Judee' A. Williamson of The Miniature Makers' Workshop.

Materials

Fabric, art foam, lace, macramé board, or a piece of ceiling tile, fine tweezers, hair spray, or Patricia Nimocks' clear acrylic sealer (matte finish) plexiglass, pleater pins, white glue for fabrics, such as Sobo, and a bed frame.

Procedure

Cut 2 pieces of fabric ½" larger than canopy or tester top. Using white glue, glue first piece of fabric onto top of frame, stretching to shape. Clip edges to accommodate curved shape of frame. Clamp canopy to a piece of plexiglass to hold it firmly in place while gluing the second layer of fabric onto frame. Trim away excess fabric.

Gluing first piece of fabric onto canopy frame.

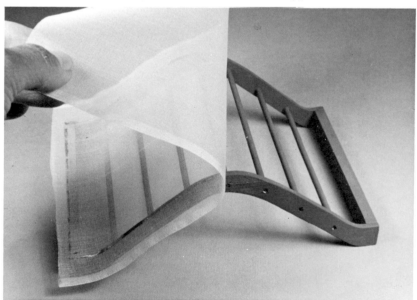

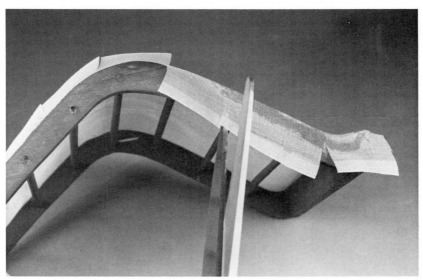

Clip edges of fabric before gluing down sides of frame.

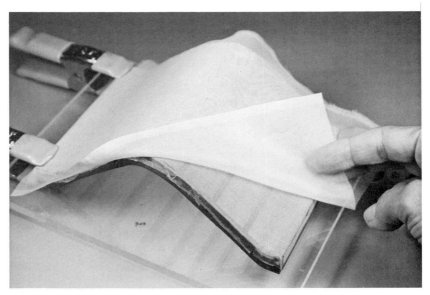

Canopy clamped to a piece of plexiglass to hold firmly in place while gluing second piece of fabric to frame.

Canopy frame after gluing and trimming excess fabric.

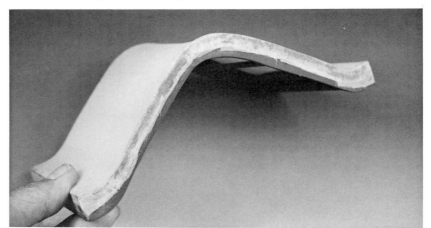

To assemble dust ruffle

The width of the dust ruffle is determined by doubling the measurement around the bed and the length by measuring the bed from the top of the bottom mattress to the floor. Do not cut your fabric with scissors. Tear it instead to the desired size. Trim the hemmed bottom with fine lace, or other trim. Machine baste 2 rows of stitching at the top of dust ruffle, ⅛" from the edge. Stitch one half the gathering line at a time. This will lessen the chance of your thread breaking when pulling the gathers. Pin onto board at the top, adjusting gathers to fit into desired length. Using tweezers, make folds, pinning each fold in place. Using a steam iron, held 1" above fabric, steam folds very gently. When fabric is dry, remove pins, tie basting threads, turn on wrong side and spray lightly with 2 coats of spray. This will hold folds in place. Pin and glue in place to bottom mattress.

Pin dust ruffle to ceiling board or macramé board, pulling threads to gather to desired width. Adjust folds with tweezers, and pin bottom in place.

Steam the folds, holding the iron 1" above your work. Do not touch fabric with the iron. Allow to dry, turn over, and spray with 2 light coats of hair spray or Patricia Nimocks' clear acrylic sealer, matte finish.

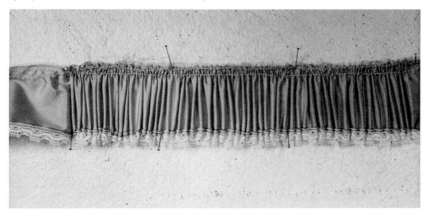

Back and side draperies

Cut back and side draperies from pattern #1, cutting 2 pieces. Place right sides of fabric facing. Stitch sides and bottom, leaving top open. Turn right side out. Press. Sew 2 rows of machine-basting stitches on dotted lines at the top indicated on pattern for gathering lines. Trim sides and bottom with lace. Pull gathering stitches to fit bed across the back and 2½" on each side. Pin to board and steam as for dust ruffle. Allow to dry, remove pins, and tie basting threads. Turn over and spray lightly with 2 thin coats of spray. Set aside.

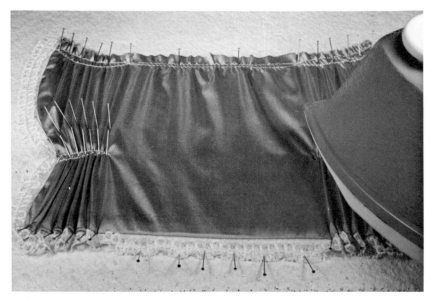

Steam back and side piece of drapery after pinning in place on board.

Back and side draperies after steaming.

Patterns for canopy bed, draperies, and bedspread.

Pattern #2   Bedspread and lining   Actual size

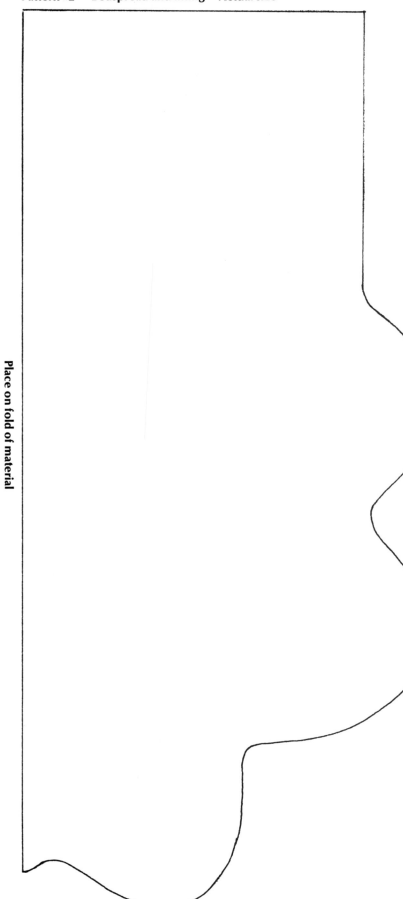

Place on fold of material

Dressing a Canopy Bed

Patterns and procedures courtesy of Judee' A. Williamson of The Miniature Makers' Workshop.

Pattern #1 for bed
Back and side draperies
(cut 2)
Actual size

Top

Place on fold of material

Bottom

QUILTED BEDSPREAD

Cut lace top and lining from pattern #2. Placing right sides facing, baste together by hand. Machine stitch, ⅛" from edge, leaving top edge open. Turn right side out and gently press. Lay a ⅛"-thick piece of art foam on back of bedcover ¼" in from edge. Using a contrasting color thread, baste stitch diagonal lines ½" apart as a guide for the quilting stitches. Following the diagonal lines, make small hand stitches ½" apart. Stitch a tiny stitch on the right side and a long one on the back side. Pull gently after each stitch to create a quilted effect. The top edge of the bedspread by the headboard does not have to be finished. This will be hidden by the satin sheet and pillows.

Cut the sheet from a piece of thin satin fabric and glue appliquéd lace cutouts on the edge to be folded down over the bedspread. The finished Hepplewhite bed described at the end of these directions did not have a full sheet. A piece of satin 3" x 8" was used to simulate a sheet.

Glue lace bedspread in place on top of mattress and glue satin sheet on top of bedspread. Make 2 pillows of satin, fill with cotton, and trim with lace. After gluing the pillows onto bed, pin and glue the bed drapery in place around canopy back and sides. Trim edge with lace. Finish by adding tiny bows to each side of the bed drapery.

In dealing with miniature making, improvising becomes a way of life: searching through old attic trunks, attending rummage sales, cutting up Aunt Tillie's old wedding gown, retrieving old kid gloves, bartering for a piece of lovely old silk or lace, in general, laying one's hands on fabrics and trimmings and bits and pieces that would be suitable for the seamstress who is bent on dressing a doll, dressing a bed, dressing a window, making a parasol or a pair of shoes. This collection of minutiae becomes a gold mine of working materials for the miniature maker.

Hand-baste lace for bedspread to lining with right sides together in preparation for machine stitching.

Right side of bedspread, with dark basting lines indicating direction of quilting stitches.

Satin sheet with cutout appliques of lace, glued in place with diluted white glue.

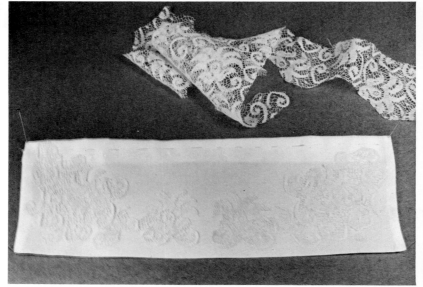

Pin drapery in place, adjusting gathering and glue.

The finished Hepplewhite bed with serpentine canopy. Made by Virginia Merrill.

BIBLIOGRAPHY

Barnes, Charles, and Blake, David. *120 Needlepoint Design Projects.* New York: Crown Publishers, Inc., 1974.

Coleman, Dorothy S., Elizabeth A., and Evelyn J. *The Collector's Book of Dolls' Clothes.* New York: Crown Publishers, Inc., 1975.

Davis, Mildred J. *The Art of Crewel Embroidery.* New York: Crown Publishers, Inc., 1962

Dreesmann, Cecile. *Samplers for Today.* New York: Van Nostrand Reinhold Company, 1972.

Felcher, Cecelia. *The Needlepoint Workbook of Traditional Designs.* New York: Hawthorn Books, Inc., 1973.

    The Complete Book of Rug Making. New York: Hawthorn Books, Inc., 1975.

Kuncior, Robert. *Mr. Godey's Ladies: Being a Mosaic of Fashions and Fancies.* Princeton, N.J.: The Pyne Press, 1971.

Liebetrau, Preben. *Oriental Rugs in Colour.* New York: Macmillan Publishing Co., 1962.

Lorentz, H. A. *A View of Chinese Rugs.* London: Routledge & Kegan Paul Ltd., 1972.

McBaine, Susan. *Miniature Needlepoint Rugs for Dollhouses.* New York: Dover Publications, Inc., 1976.

Molesworth, H. D., and Browne, Kenworthy John. *Three Centuries of Furniture in Color.* New York: The Viking Press, 1969.

187

Rome, Carol Cheney, and Devlin, Georgia French. *A New Look at Needlepoint*. New York: Crown Publishers, Inc., 1972.

Roth, Charlene Davis. *Dressing Dolls*. New York: Crown Publishers, Inc., 1976.

Ruedin-Gans, E. *The Connoisseur's Guide to Oriental Carpets*. Rutland, Vt.: Charles E. Tuttle Co., 1971.

Scobey, Joan. *Rugs & Wall Hangings*. New York: The Dial Press, 1974.

The Tiffany Studios. *Antique Chinese Rugs*. Rutland, Vt.: Charles E. Tuttle Co., 1969.

Weeks, Jenne G., and Treganowan, Donald. *Rugs and Carpets of Europe and the Western World*. Philadelphia, Pa.: Chilton Book Co., 1969.

Wilson, Erica. *Erica Wilson's Embroidery Book*. New York: Charles Scribner's Sons, 1973.

SUPPLY SOURCES

Please send a long SASE (self-addressed stamped envelope) for reply.

Alice's Annex
Cyrena K. Gouge, Proprietor
P.O. Box 681
Devon, Pennsylvania 19333

Hand-braided rugs, shaker furniture, colonial pieces, and complete rooms

Appleton Bros. of London
West Main Road
Little Compton, Rhode Island 02837

Crewel wool for petit point rugs. Wholesale only

Art Needlework of Georgia, Inc.
8 North Rhodes Center N.W.
Atlanta, Georgia 30309

Appleton yarn, DMC embroidery floss, Soie d'Alger "à la Coquille"—French silk, Pearsall's English silk. No price list or catalogue, but do stop in.

Bauder-Pine, Ltd.
Side Door Antiques and Miniatures
133 West Maple Avenue
Langhorne, Pennsylvania 19047

Crewel bed sets, pillows, curtains, sofas, chairs. Rugs. Appliqué bed sets

Mrs. Frank Bears
592 South Pelham Street
Welland, Ontario, Canada L3C3C6

Needlepoint rugs

Barbara Bergrath
300 Woodbury Road
Woodbury, New York 11797

Custom-made rugs and pillows

Betty's Doll House
Cates Plaza Suite 117
375 Pharr Road N.E.
Atlanta, Georgia 30305

Needlepoint rugs

Big As A Dot
5400 Astor Lane, Apt. 212
Rolling Meadows, Illinois 60008

Parasols, bonnets, shoes, leather saddles, bridles, and other handcrafted items

Boutique Margot
26 West 54th Street
New York, New York 10019

Silk gauze #24, 29, 38, 48, 58, DMC embroidery floss, Zwicky silk, Appleton yarn, even-weave fabric

189

Calico Miniatures
c/o Leon's Studio
70 Witherspoon Street
Princeton, New Jersey 08540

*Needlepoint rugs, fancy dressed beds,
upholstered furniture*

Cantitoe Corners
36 West 20th Street
New York, New York 10011

*Do-it-yourself quilt kits, do-it-yourself
bed kits*

Carter's Creations
13860 Midlothian Turnpike
Midlothian, Virginia 23113

Exclusively designed miniature carpets

Chestnut Hill Studio, Ltd.
Box 907
Taylors, South Carolina 29687

*Upholstered items; draperies; braided,
handwoven, and needlepoint rugs.
$3.00 for fully illustrated catalogue*

Elsa T. Cose
1207 Plainfield Avenue
Plainfield, New Jersey 07060

*Pearsall's Filo floss, Zwicky floss, #10
crewel embroidery needles*

Cottage Crafts
149 Lancaster Pike
West of Route 401
Malvern, Pennsylvania 19355

Rug embroidery supplies

Crafty Woman
Route 34
Colts Neck, New Jersey 07722

*DMC embroidery floss, #24 mesh
canvas*

Create Your Own
Box 393
Peapack, New Jersey 07977

*Needlepoint rug kits, crewel kits, fabric
design kits*

Crewel By Cathy, Inc.
P.O. Box 291
Granby, Connecticut 06035

Custom House
West Townsend, Massachusetts 01474

Crewel kits

Dearring-Tracy Ltd.
50 Central Park West
New York, New York 10023

*Exceptionally fine musical instruments,
custom-made dolls*

June Dole Cross Stitch Kits
1280 North Stone Street
West Suffield, Connecticut 06093

*Cross-stitch sampler kits. Also available
for non-sewers—completed samplers*

Dolls Restored
Anne Marie Zobel
P.O. Box 252
Manchester, Vermont 05255

The Enchanted Doll House
Route 7
Manchester Center, Vermont 05255

*Needlepoint and woven rugs, crewel
embroidered bed sets*

Renee Farber
17 Dorchester Drive
Monsey, New York 10952

*#22 mesh canvas, #44 silk gauze, DMC
embroidery floss, Appleton crewel
wool*

Margaret Finch, N.I.A.D.A.
106 Liberty Avenue
New Rochelle, New York 10805

*Fine art dolls, one-of-a-kind creations
of distinction and beauty*

Mary Fry
610 Springfield Avenue
Summit, New Jersey 07901

*Appleton yarn, Zwicky silk, silk gauze
#34, #40, #44, and other embroidery
supplies. Catalogue available, $1.00*

Lillian Gaines
212 South 6th Street
Independence, Kansas 67301

Handwoven miniature coverlets

Nancy A. Hebner
Ninham Road
R.D. 3
Carmel, New York 10512

Miniature Oriental rug reproductions

Jim Holmes
16 Rand Place
Bedford, Massachusetts 01730

*Colonial miniatures, telescopes, rifles,
muskets, masks*

Jelly Beans
Needlepoint Studio
524 Camino del Monte Sol
Santa Fe, New Mexico 87501

*Canvas mesh #18, #24, silk gauze #30,
#40, #54. DMC embroidery floss, silk
thread, Marlitt rayon, yarn palettes,
even-weave fabric for cross-stitch and
crewel. Brochure available.*

Judy's Little-uns
920 Central Avenue
Ocean City, New Jersey 08226

*Handmade dollhouse people, fully
dressed*

Kay's Creations
2086 Fairwood Lane N.E.
Atlanta, Georgia 30345

*Miniature needlepoint, hand-painted
canvas rugs, bellpulls*

Knit Wit Shop
26 Beechwood Road
Summit, New Jersey 07901

*Canvas mesh #22, #24, DMC
embroidery floss*

La Petite Miniatures
Village Square Route 4
Bergen Mall
Paramus, New Jersey 07652

*Handmade Victorian beds, fully
dressed. Bonnets, hats, purses,
handmade dolls and clothing*

The Little Needlepoint Shop
Jean P. Wernentin
830 State Street
Bettendorf, Iowa 52722

*Canvas mesh #24, silk gauze #24, #40.
DMC embroidery floss, Appleton yarn,
linen thread, Marlitt, French silk, even-
weave fabric*

Virginia Manning
8001 Navajo Street
Philadelphia, Pennsylvania

*Petit point rugs and accessories made to
your specifications*

Mini-Bazaar
400 Westminster Avenue
Newport Beach, California 92663

Rugs and rug kits

Mini-Magic Carpet
3675 Reed Road
Columbus, Ohio 43220

Oriental-designed needlepoint rugs, completely finished or in kits

Miniature Makers Workshop
677 South Eton
Birmingham, Michigan 48012

Fully dressed canopy beds, upholstered chairs, chaises longues

The Miniature Rug Bug
2089 Olive Avenue
Lakewood, Ohio 44107

Braided rugs, hand-crocheted bedspreads and canopy sets

The Mouse Hole
111 Eagle Rock Avenue
Roseland, New Jersey 07068

Braided rugs; stools, benches, and chairs covered with petit point

Janice Naibert
16590 Emory Lane
Rockville, Maryland 20853

Laces, flowers, ribbons, and assorted trims

Needlegraph
P.O. Box 186
Huntington Station
Dix Hills, New York 11746

Graph paper

Needleworks in Miniature
Barbara Cosgrove
P.O. Box 28041
Atlanta, Georgia 30328

Museum quality rug kits and finished models. Send $2.00 and long SASE

The Needle and Shuttle
104 South Main Street
North Wales, Pennsylvania 19454

Needlepoint supplies, kits, silk gauze, X-Acto Tidewater Collection of Oriental Rug Kits

Carol Nordell, N.I.A.D.A.
368 East 5th Street
Mt. Vernon, New York 10553

Hand-modeled characters and period people, made to order. A "how-to" book for making a miniature Nutcracker Ballet: $6.95 per copy, plus 75¢ for mailing. N.Y. residents please add appropriate sales tax.

Judith Ohanian
18336 Western Avenue
Homewood, Illinois 60430

Custom-designed petit point rugs worked in 28 stitches to the inch

Hazel Pearson Handicrafts
Rosemead, California 91770

Art Foam

The Pixie Shop
Dept. NN-3
5580 Colt Drive
Longmont, Colorado 80501

Miniature linens, crewel pictures, tiny print fabrics. 35¢ and long SASE for brochure

Gloria B. Richardson
P.O. Box 152
Bay Head, New Jersey 08742

Finely braided rugs, shaker rugs, and petit point rugs

Susan Merrill Richardson
9 Everett Avenue
Winchester, Massachusetts 01890

Custom designed petit point of distinction. Backgammon boards, rugs, Bargello chairs, fire screens, and stools. Send $1.00 and long SASE for brochure

Royal School of Needlework
25 Princess Gate
London SW7

Needlework supplies

Doreen Sinnett Designs
Newport Beach, California 92663

Mini-Hooker

Susan Sirkis
11909 Blue Spruce
Reston, Virginia 22091

Exquisitely made and dressed dolls

Marian K. Stannard
100 Franklin Street
3D-12A
Morristown, New Jersey 07960

Miniature petit point designs on even-weave fabric, suitable for pillows, pictures, fire screens, and greeting cards

Stitch Witchery
Denbrook Village
P.O. Box N
Denville, New Jersey 07834

DMC embroidery floss, Appleton yarn, silk gauze #36, Canvas mesh #22, #24, Pearsall's silk, Fawcett linen thread, even-weave fabric

Summit Electrical Supply Co.
520 Morris Avenue
Summit, New Jersey 07901

Dazor lamps for magnification

Lorrie Sweatt's Dollhouse
at the Greenbrier Hotel
White Sulphur Springs
West Virginia 24986

Dressed dolls, custom-made rugs, watercolor paintings, clocks

Paige Thornton
3216 Clairmont Road
Atlanta, Georgia 30329

Victorian crib, old dolls, petit point pillows, rugs, and other fine miniatures

Thumbelina Needlework Shop
1685 Copenhagen Drive
Solvang, California 93463

Needlework and embroidery supplies, silk gauze #22, #30,#40, #26, tapestry needles for petit point

Victoria's Doll House
Creek Road
Rancocas Woods, New Jersey 08060

Needlepoint rugs made to order or do-it-yourself rug kits

Harry Whalon
1550 Hudson Court
Orlando, Florida 32808

Petit point rug designs and kits

Whitehead & Associates
P.O. Box 278 Route 413
Newtown, Pennsylvania 18940

Knitted and crocheted bedspreads, rug kits, samplers, crewel items

Pat Wyeth
"On a Small Scale"
168 Washington Place
Ridgewood, New Jersey 07450

Kid gloves, shoes, purses, and bonnets

Cookie Ziemba
5 York Court
New City, New York 10956

Petit point worked on frame, yarn caddy, purses, bellpulls

INDEX

Pages in italics refer to illustrations.